CRISIS OF FAITH

CRISIS OF FAITH

*The Religious Psychology
of Adolescence*

PIERRE BABIN

HERDER AND HERDER

1963
HERDER AND HERDER NEW YORK
232 Madison Avenue, New York 16, N.Y.

First edition 1963
Second impression 1964

Original edition "*Les jeunes et la foi,*" Lyons, Edition du Chalet, 1960. Translation and adaptation by Eva Fleischner, The Grail.

Nihil obstat:
                Patrick A. Barry
                Censor Librorum
Imprimatur:
                † Robert F. Joyce
                Bishop of Burlington
                June 14, 1963

CONTENTS

FOREWORD

It is not an exaggeration to say that until now the modern catechetical renewal in English-speaking countries has been without a religious-psychological dimension. Studies abound, largely done under Protestant auspices, in which the response of children or adolescents to situations that have overtones of religion is explored. Aside from the regrettable fact that the Catholic catechist goes largely unaware of them, there is the further fact that most of these studies are not religiously oriented in a strict sense, but are concerned to discover a correlation between ethical behavior and church-school attendance or something of the sort.

The studies done by English-speaking Catholic scholars whether in university faculties or by way of private research are often at the same level. The reason for this is in neither case, Protestant or Catholic, the lack of religious concern on the part of the scholars. Prescinding from those cases where they have real difficulty in identifying what are the concerns of revealed religion—being basically moralists who are also believers—Christian psychologists usually have not explored the Christian message with any of the thoroughness that has marked their inquiry into human behavior. In sum, the mature psychologist who has set himself seriously to master the implications of God's revelation, and the theologian-catechist who knows modern psychology well, whether depth, Freudian, Jungian or other, are two types of scholar that have not yet come to the fore.

Immediately one has said this, the names of Catholics who are generally oriented to the need for a psychology of faith come to mind. Most are Europeans whose works are available in translation; the proposition in any case holds: they are more prone to have an orientation to the question than to have grappled scientifically with the problems of religious psychology.

It would be gratifying to say that the present work represents an absolute breakthrough in the world of English-speaking catechetics but such is not the case. The author is a man of France; he is a catechist whose orientation is psychological, not one deep in both theology and psychology; he has written a volume based largely on the researches of others. Despite all this he has provided an English readership, through the offices of his professional collaborator Miss Eva Fleischner, with a volume that has no exact forerunner; it is a unique contribution on any accounting. The adolescent of his concern is a person approaching age twenty: for the most part he is one who will attend college (we use American terminology) or is intellectually capable of doing so.

Catechists in the United States who labor in elementary and secondary school situations are coming to realize the strong pull their students experience away from fidelity to Christ. What was described by these catechists in hushed tones a few decades ago as an isolated scandal they now recognize as a widespread phenomenon, namely departure in the adolescent period from the faith of early youth. This crisis of faith is intimately related to the quality of catechetical instruction given from earliest childhood through the high school years. It is equally related to the dynamic quality of parish liturgy or to its opposite, apathy in worship at the diocesan and parish levels. The question is openly discussed in a way it was not twenty or even ten years ago. No longer is the secular spirit with its appeal to the passions identified as the sole enemy; the failures in catechetics and pastoral care are coming to be seen as equally inimical to the formation of mature Christians in the period of late adolescence.

Those who know Father Babin for the prophetic teacher he is—a blend of profundity, insight, and Gallic verve—will enjoy a fresh encounter with him in these pages. Those who have not experienced his writing through the pages of *Lumen Vitae* or *Religious Education* will surely say: "He knows the modern scene and he knows young people." This volume points the way to the dozens of serious studies we need on the central problem of adolescence: can the young Christian of today really believe?

GERARD S. SLOYAN

TRANSLATOR'S NOTE

A number of changes from the original French have been made in this edition in order to facilitate its use for American readers: Several references to French sources difficult to locate have been omitted. Wherever possible English editions of the works cited are given. A few editorial notes were added by the translator.— More extensive changes were made in the chapter on *Today's Youth*, where several American statistics and sources appear in the body of the text as well as in the footnotes, in place of French references. They have not been specifically identified, since the substitutions are evident.—All these changes were made in close collaboration and consultation with the author.

I wish to express my gratitude to Fr. George Hagmeier, C.P.S., of the Paulist Institute for Religious Research, for his valuable advice concerning adaptations to the American scene; to Miss Anne Finnan, Librarian at Fordham University, and Miss Carol Donahoe, of the Grailville Department of Religious Education, for helping me locate American sources; and most of all to Miss Carole Spearin, of the Grail National Secretariat, whose patient reading of the manuscript and capable literary advice made possible my completion of the translation.

EVA FLEISCHNER
Grailville
Loveland, Ohio

Three Ways of Seeing

To know someone is to enter into a relationship with him. When two people first meet they are strangers to each other, there is distance between them. This distance must be bridged, so that they can cross over and meet. Two persons can come to know each other only if there is an encounter, and if certain contacts and ties are established between them. We know this from daily experience.

An encounter can, however, occur at levels of varying depths. What kind of knowledge or—this amounts to the same thing—what kind of encounter is involved in religious psychology, in the psychology of the life of faith?

There is one way of seeing which we might call superficial knowledge or "surface" psychology. For example, Jack has lost his way in a strange town. He looks questioningly at the passers-by, hoping to find someone who can give him directions. At last he stops a workman who seems to be from that part of town and asks him the way.

In this passing meeting with a stranger Jack depended upon his sense of psychology. A question and an answer, a moment of noticing each other, of willingness to help. Their paths have barely crossed, there was no dialogue.

They remain nameless to each other. Each continues on his road in the secrecy of his individuality.

Two factors entered into this meeting: an instinctive, elementary psychology on the natural level, so superficial that we can hardly speak of psychology here; and a superficial contact between two people, devoid of personal relationship.

There is a second, deeper, way of seeing: with greater human knowledge, or natural scientific psychology. Thus, a sick person consults a psychiatrist. The psychiatrist questions him at length, places him under observation and puts him through various tests. After several examinations the doctor has accumulated a file, which records with the greatest possible accuracy his patient's I.Q., exhaustion threshold, emotional reactions, talents, weaknesses, etc.

At this stage the psychological knowledge is obviously much more advanced, it has become a real science. The doctor has gained accurate and sure knowledge about everything that can quantitatively be measured in his patient, and this is precisely the object of science.

At this point, however, we might raise an objection. Since it is a matter of quantitative evaluation, can we really speak of human knowledge, of personal encounter? We can, to the extent to which the doctor has encountered the person of his patient through the material realities he was studying. And this encounter was all the easier to achieve because the material realities were very close to the mystery of person of the sick man. It is true that clinical examination and study of natural psychology can remain on the level of a purely material evaluation; observing psychic

phenomena and discovering in them the relations of cause
and effect is the privileged domain of natural psychology
and does not itself involve personal relationships. In actual
fact, however, we find two elements here:

First, an authentic and scientific psychology, proportionate to the gravity of the medical case. This knowledge is
still on the level of natural techniques and outside the explicit context of the perspectives of faith. At the same time,
a genuine human encounter took place, to the degree in
which two persons have become aware of each other—
more or less deeply, more or less permanently.

The third way of seeing searches the depths: it is with
Christian knowledge, or religious psychology in the perspective of faith. When the Christian looks at man, the light of
his faith does not in any way lessen the seriousness and
weight of the human phenomena he has scientifically ex-
amined. For the believer as for the unbeliever, a fact remains a fact; the link that relates two facts persists, and
gives rise to a scientific law. At this level no difference is
possible—provided, of course, that it is a matter of science
rather than mere hypothesis. Believer and unbeliever, therefore, meet on the common ground of natural and rational
science.

The Christian's view, however, will go far beyond the
natural dimension of the facts and laws that have been
established, without in the least altering their consistency.
Through his faith the believer enters into a new way of
seeing and knowing.

Let us make this clear by comparing the ways of seeing
of two men. An architect and a passer-by both look at the

same building. Compared to the passer-by, the architect's
way of looking is much deeper and richer. He perceives relationships of line and materials, of the whole and of parts.
He senses the possibilities of enlarging or remodeling the
building; perhaps, also, he notices weak spots which escape
the casual view of the other. In short, we can say that the
architect sees reality in a much greater depth and shading,
so that a whole world of meanings, possibilities, and dangers lies open before him.

The same is true when we compare the vision of the believer with that of the unbeliever. Both may be scientists;
both may practice an authentic scientific psychology. The
believer, however, can, without losing any of his natural
objectivity, give new interpretation and meaning to things.
He can open up dangers or possibilities which are, naturally
speaking, hidden from the gaze of the unbeliever.

Our perspective throughout this book will be that of the
believer. We shall look at man not merely in his natural
dimension, but with the new and clear vision which our
life in Christ gives us. The first generations of Christians
did not cease to thank the Father for the grace of *illumination*, for the knowledge which had been bestowed upon
them in Jesus Christ: a joyful and serene knowledge of the
"things that are above," of the destiny of man and of the
cosmos. "Blessed are the eyes that see what you see."

The Key to a New Vision of Man

When a young girl meets a young man whom she loves,
she knows him not only as he is in himself, but also in rela-

INTRODUCTION 15

tion to herself. She knows that if he accepts her love she will help him to become a happy and better person. To put it another way: she knows herself in relation to him.

So too with Christ. Upon coming into this world, sent by the Father, Christ knows Himself in relation to this world; and He knows man in fullness and in truth, as a being that will be transformed, or that can be transformed, by His presence and action.

Jesus is well aware of the meaning of His words when He compares the earth to soil waiting to receive the seed. By coming into this world He calls it to a higher, to a supernatural existence: He calls the soil to enter into the composition of the plant. This is henceforth to be the true earth.

In Scripture the world is compared to a bride who is waiting for her bridegroom. When Jesus comes, He comes as the Bridegroom of this world, as the one who will perfect and complete man. That is why He constantly affirms with absolute authority throughout the Gospel: "I am the Resurrection, the Life, the Truth. . . ."

Jesus does not come in order to make man serve Him, still less to use him, or to exploit him for selfish ends, to "alienate" him.[1] To do so would make no sense for God. A creator does not alienate his creation, he brings it into existence. Jesus Christ came for this, and only for this: to give man eternal life. He came in the fullness of time in order to bring man to perfection in the glory of God. In

[1] To *alienate*: in the sense in which Nietzsche uses the term. He accuses God of separating Himself from His creation, of "estranging" His creation.

the words of St. Irenaeus, "the glory of God is man fully alive."

This, then, is how Jesus Christ sees man: as a being destined to be saved, transformed, supernaturalized, without losing here below the least fraction of his humanity, without renouncing any part of his fleshly substance. The true man, the really successful man, is Jesus Christ. This is the future, when "God will be all in all."

In this perspective we begin to suspect the extraordinary depth of Christ's way of seeing, and the weight of His human encounters. When Christ looks at man He does not merely touch him superficially. He encounters him, He "realizes" him in the literal meaning of the word, that is to say, He makes him real. He gives his existence a weightiness which man cannot acquire by himself. When Christ looks at man He calls him, raises him, up, or rather, He "re-surrects" him. He makes him enter, by grace, into the new world of Easter.

What is the key to a Christian vision of man? It is nothing else than a share in Christ's own way of seeing. It is our faith in the Incarnation of the Son of God. It is the assurance that, in the Pasch of the Lord, all earthly realities have been saved in hope, and await the full revelation of glory. The secret of a new vision of reality lies in the relationship we manage to establish between human, natural and psychological realities, and the Lord Jesus Christ, who is the Alpha and the Omega, the beginning and the end of the universe.

Thus to the believer who sees to the heart of things, man appears only in his relation to the Son of God. We know, in faith, that this is the true texture of reality. To believe is to see clearly and to know that "these things are certain and true" (Apoc. 21:5).

Meaning and Scope of Our Study

It is in this perspective of Christian realism that we shall study the evolution of the life of faith of adolescents and young people. We shall relate the facts, pointing up the constant factors which can be observed objectively, and showing their meaning in the light of Revelation. We shall point out the ambiguities as well as the possibilities and dangers that are latent in them.

The subject of this study is central to religious psychology, since our concern is the fundamental relationship of man to God. Moreover, the study of the life of faith of adolescents will frequently involve a more general study of their entire spiritual life. And since everything in man is interrelated, a brief analysis of his childhood, and of his evolution toward adulthood, will permit us to situate the meaning of adolescence in a wider context. Finally, after we have described a number of characteristics of today's youth in their confrontation with faith, we shall arrive at some catechetical and pedagogical conclusions.

We shall frequently refer to an inquiry made among some 2000 adolescents[2]; only rarely, however, shall we use it in its scientific form. This book is, rather, the fruit of long experience with adolescents. Over the years this ex-

[2] P. Babin and the Center for Research in Religious Adolescent Psychology, Dieu et l'adolescent (Lyon: Editions du Chalet, 1963).

perience has benefited from the work of several research
teams and from discussion with other educators. We have
drawn as well on numerous written or oral testimonies,
and made use of the findings of various surveys.

The adolescents referred to are usually French, and belong to a wide variety of social backgrounds. If the greater
part of written testimonies comes from students (of both
public and Catholic schools), we have taken care to go
beyond this school environment either by direct contact
with rural or working-class young people, or by consulting
specialists in these fields.

Finally, we shall quote extracts from recent novels or
autobiographies. The deliberately frequent use made of
such material may come as a surprise. To us, however, these
texts seem to express in striking literary form things which
the mass of young people live or feel only instinctively and
vaguely.

Having thus widened as much as possible the scope of
our points of departure, we shall stand a fair chance of
going beyond the purely sociological factors in order to
come to universally valid psychological realities.

The topic of this study has, of course, a special relevance
for educators, since men of today—especially young people
—have a craving to be seen in their true being and for
themselves. They want to be listened to, to be taken seriously. If we know how to look at them they will listen
to us; but how can we expect them to listen if, in pretend-
ing to speak to them, we talk only to ourselves?

They abhor the person who speaks without love, the
person who "theorizes," who "loves to hear himself talk."

Woe to the educator who speaks words devoid of love, who does not address them to "someone." They will not listen to him, they will not enter into a true exchange. For he has not addressed them personally. He has betrayed man.

Woe, too, to him whose words are empty because, in betraying man he has also betrayed God, this God "who knows what is in the heart of man," this God whose Word has become flesh in order that man might enter into communion with Him.

In order to call man in his innermost depths and kindle in him a dialogue with his Lord, the educator must first of all make his own the vision of Christ. If "no man has ever spoken as This Man," it is because no man ever saw as He saw. Whoever is called, in the footsteps of Christ, to "speak God" to men, must necessarily take his way of seeing from Christ.

It is in the hope of assisting the growth of such a way of seeing that we publish this study. Over and above analyzing various situations, we hope to show the dynamic movement of man's psychological development and its meaning in relation to the transcendent world of Revelation. Through this the educator will perhaps learn to see more truly—with the clarity of faith and the firmness of hope—this soil in which he is to sow the seed.

PART ONE

THE PSYCHOLOGICAL DATA

CHAPTER ONE

THE ACT OF FAITH AND THE ADOLESCENT

The adolescent is like a connecting link in the religious development of man and in the believer's growth in the life of faith. Specialists have not failed to study this stage, which touches the stable worlds of childhood and of adulthood, connecting them both.

Psychologists who study the adolescents' mentality speak in this context of a religious and moral crisis, of conversion, of a change in outlook, of taking a strong and often definitive stand. They stress the subjective development of man at grips with natural religion.[1]

These psychological phenomena, which can easily be verified, acquire a special form and dimension in the case of the believer. Here, the religious crisis no longer appears as an alternative between the acceptance or rejection of natural

[1] F. L. Guittard, *L'évolution religieuse des adolescents* (Paris: Spes, 1952), pp. 72–3 ff., where the author poses the question. According to E. D. Starbuck, "Boys who experience intensely the *definite crisis* (a severe and definitive conversion) do so around the age of 17–18. Some psychologists who have studied the adolescent use the word "conversion" in the sense of a "religious experience that is intensified by the need for a profound revision of conduct." According to them this conversion has three peaks—at the ages of 12, 16 and 19.

religion, but as a Yes or No on the part of man to an objective Revelation and a historical event—more precisely, to the Person of Jesus Christ. In a profound Christian conversion man opens himself to God in the Person of Jesus Christ.

If in both cases the psychological phenomena seem at first to be similar, their inner meaning obviously differs greatly. We shall, therefore, go beyond a merely natural examination of the facts, and attempt to analyze at this point the adolescent's religious crisis in the light of faith.

The act of faith is not an irrational act with no other norms than man's moods or subjective religious experiences. It is an act which requires certain objective elements.

In order that I can believe in someone, this person must first of all reveal himself to me[2] through signs, acts, or events which can be tangibly recognized. Jesus worked numerous signs that bore witness to Him, "so that, believing, we may have life in His name."

The Church has always insisted on the objective reality and on the actuality of these signs: the proclamation of the Message and the coherence of Revelation (which, according to St. Thomas, is the "great miracle"), the presence of the Church, physical and moral miracles, etc.

Obviously, these objective factors alone will not suffice to bring about the act of faith. I don't believe in someone simply because he exists. I must also, from the depth of my heart, become open to his being. I must be well disposed

[2] "Credibility is the property of a testimony and, consequently, not the evidence of an idea, but the *manifestation of a person*." Jean Mouroux, *I Believe* (New York: Sheed & Ward, 1959), p. 57.

toward him. These are the subjective elements of the act of faith.

Thus grace works on a double level: from without, and from within. There is the *presentation of the signs of faith* (objective element) on the one hand, and also the *indispensable openness* (subjective element). The same Spirit who is present in the signs in which the Person of the Living God reveals Himself enters into the vision of the man who seeks God and communicates to him that hidden light which will at last enable him to decipher the signs. The act of faith is born from the operation of grace on these two levels.

In the course of man's life this act of faith takes forms and dimensions which correspond to his psychological development. Thus, a child's act of faith cannot have the same degree of knowledge and freedom as that of the adult. Only little by little, as he matures psychologically, will the act of faith come to include all the wealth latent in the human person.

This should not surprise us. As Fr. Liégé has noted: "If man lives his life in a personal history, if the lesson of the human experience of childhood, youth, maturity and old age is so full of meaning, if there is given to each man an average life-span which goes beyond adolescence—why should we think it strange that God gives to man time to progress toward supernatural maturity in a rhythm that follows his human maturing? . . . In order to bestow His full measure, God waits until man is wide awake."[3]

[3] A. Liégé, O.P., *Adultes dans le Christ* (Brussels, 1958), pp. 9–10.

Adolescence marks a crisis in the process of human growth, a turning point which deserves to be studied in detail. Before describing this process of maturing, however, let us consider the actual presence of the signs of faith in the world of young people today, and their objective attitudes toward them.

Let us ask, first: are the signs of faith available to today's adolescents? Secondly: are the subjective attitudes that make possible the act of faith (particularly the sense of the sacred, the need for Redemption, and a good moral life) present in the adolescent—and if so, under what form? Does the psychology of the adolescent foster in general those attitudes which are a prerequisite for faith?[4]

Or again: does the climate of our time on the one hand, and that of adolescent psychology on the other, help him to become open to the commitment of faith?[5] To give an example: his instinctive fascination with absolutes and his thirst for justice will obviously influence profoundly his free subjective disposition in the act of faith.

Are the Signs of Faith Available to Adolescents?

"In order that our faith might be a homage conformed to the desire of reason, God deigned to add to the interior

---

[4] We are concerned not only with the adolescent in general, but with today's adolescent.

[5] We carefully distinguish here the free disposition of the subject (the adolescent) from that which conditions it. Whether man lives in a shack or mansion will affect favorably or unfavorably his disposition, his attitude toward the call of God. The extent of this conditioning varies; man is still free.

helps of the Holy Spirit external proofs of His Revelation:
divine facts which . . . constitute the sure signs of Revelation and which are, moreover, adapted to the intellect of
all men" (First Vatican Council).

These "divine facts—in the first place miracles and
prophecies," are divine guarantees given to man, rational,
objective guarantees of the commitment of faith. These
same facts, moreover, are "a test of man's subjective attitudes and oblige him to declare of which spirit he is."[6]

Christ commanded His disciples to perform "signs." In
sending them out on their mission He even makes explicit
the quality of the signs they are to perform for the sake of
the Kingdom of God which they are to proclaim (Luke
9:1–7). These signs are not simply recorded in history
books as souvenirs—although this has indeed some value
for the intellect—but they are renewed today. The Church
"speaks" Christ. Today as yesterday she is the sign of
Christ: through her physical miracles, but also through
the witness of Christians whose lives pose a question for the
man who is starved for a full human existence; in short,
through all her words, acts and doings.[7]

[6] A. Liégé, Initiation théologique, III, 484.
[7] These are moral miracles in so far as they reveal a way of life
which surpasses the natural powers of man's intellect and ability.
Some examples: a Christian community, or a group of young people
living together in joy, friendship, universal brotherhood and prayer.
Or—a young girl who has just received her Ph.D. in philosophy
takes the first train home in order to enter a religious order. Such a
way of "making a success of one's life" poses a question which reveals a dimension that transcends man. Or—in a certain factory a
Christian woman who is always cheerful and ready to help arouses in
another woman the question of faith. "I don't see," she says to her,
"how you can be happy all the time. . . ."

We may ask whether these signs are available to adolescents in our time. In order to answer this question we must lay aside a certain concept of the actual visibility of signs, or of the geographic presence of the Church in a given place.

Even in Christian countries where these signs exist and where the Church enjoys a certain standing (through the parish, press, school system, etc.), one is struck by the absence of the signs of faith in many spheres of modern life. True, it is certainly not desirable that TV, sports, or the business world should cease to be secular activities and become "clericalized"; but what witness to the Gospel is being given by the followers of Christ in all the deep layers of our modern world? To quote a Marxist: "We are not interested in knowing whether Christ really existed, we don't care. The only thing that interests us is, Where are the Christians? What are they doing?"

Numerous studies reveal that large numbers of adolescents today live without any signs of faith.[8] Not that the Church is geographically absent from their environment; but she is indeed all too absent from the great spheres of human life from which young people draw their most vital strength: from the world of science, technology, leisure and work. The "salt of the Gospel" is lacking. The Church is not even a source of worry to them: she is simply not present.

An analysis of the study mentioned above showed that the decisive factors for the adolescents' faith were the

[8] Journées Nationales de l'Enseignement Religieux, 1959; preliminary surveys. Cf. the special issue of the "Documentation Catéchistique."

presence or the absence of the signs of faith in their every-day environment. True, they rated the sacramental life first, with an average of 30.6%. Nevertheless, they felt that the presence of friends, of people committed to the apostolate, of a Christian environment, were the strongest supports for their faith:

pre-adolescents	29%
adolescents	26%
late adolescents	25.5%

A disillusioned engineering student writes: "What is so difficult is that I am all alone, I have no friend with whom I can discuss religion. . . ."

Before we criticize any one method, we must denounce the real absence of the signs of the Gospel. The Catholic school, when it is truly Catholic, makes the signs visible and forces the students to take sides.[9] But where are the signs of faith in our institutes of technology and secular universities, in our vocational schools, etc.?

Another problem arises from the fact that the human signs which proclaim God can be so inadequate, false, or distorted that they lose their power as sign. Thus, if I shake someone's hand with bandaged fingers, the one to whom I show this sign of friendship is likely to be more aware of my bandaged hand than of the meaning of the gesture. It takes very little at times to distort or disfigure a sign.

[9] An inquiry among young people shows the value of the Catholic school in making present the signs of faith. Students are in general forced to take sides. It is true that the signs of faith are often ill adapted to their mentality, which leads to sharp criticism. But in spite of their rebellion, these adolescents are challenged by the Church.

It is in this sense that Pope John XXIII dared to say to the Roman seminarians of the Greek College on June 4, 1959: "When the Church has been healthily modernized and rejuvenated, then she will be able to say to our separated brethren: Come to us!"

We know, moreover, that although the great historical signs of Revelation—prophecies, miracles, Christ's Resurrection, the witness of the first martyrs, etc.—retain an absolute value, they require contemporary trappings to guarantee their authenticity and make possible their transmission. It is through a Christian who is joyful and passionately vowed to justice that a pagan today can understand the historical sign of Easter. It is through the whole Church alive today that the books which tell of the Resurrection of Jesus can have the function of sign for modern men.

Let us suppose an impossibility. If one day there were to be no longer any trace of the church on earth, the books which tell of Christ's Resurrection would be nothing but signs of a Christ who is dead; that is, the account of the Resurrection would be nothing more than a *legend*. We know very well, however, that this is nonsense, that it cannot happen. When Christ promises to be with His Church until the end of time He does not make some kind-hearted promise which is extrinsic to His being, but He simply *speaks His Resurrection*.

The actual sign of Christ is the Church today: it is all Christians, truly illuminated and transformed by the dynamism of the Resurrection of Jesus.

Many atheists do not deny that Christ was an extraordinary man; what they do deny is the meaning and power of

His Resurrection because (so they say) these are not
apparent among Christians. In their eyes Christ cannot
have a value which transcends history, because Christians
today no longer exert an effect on the world. Therefore
Christ was nothing but a moment in history.

It is true that even when the signs do exist in their
fullness, they may not necessarily be recognized in all
their meaning; for that meaning is "not of flesh and blood,"
but of God. Nevertheless, we should constantly examine
ourselves on the quality of this "epiphany" for which we
are responsible here on earth. Christians (and educators
in particular) should make a continuous examination of
conscience, in the tranquil yet challenging light of the
Holy Spirit: are they being faithful to Him whom they
signify? Have they sufficiently penetrated into *His Truth*
and into the unique effectiveness of His Resurrection?

Let us underline at this point certain lacks which became
apparent in the course of our study:

1) In certain situations the explicit signs of Revelation
have lost much of their force of appeal, because they are
either inadequate or distorted. Many religious institutions,
for instance, are too concerned with a natural morality
that is strongly Jansenist and voluntarist. This is evident
in their preoccupation with the problem of purity, in the
insistence on certain religious practices and on an out-
moded discipline.[10] All this is obtained at the expense of a
Christian life lived in joy, in peace, in the service of others,
in commitment to justice and to charity.

[10] Cf. P. Babin, *Dieu et l'adolescent*, the chapter on the sense of
God in different scholastic environments.

2) The complementary testimonies of religious (who embody the eschatological aspect of the faith), of lay people (who embody commitment to the world in charity), and of priests (who bring God to men from "on-high") are inadequately related and have little power as signs for young people. In too many institutions the witness given by the religious appears too exclusive and not compelling enough: too exclusive, because the witness of the laity is not stressed; not compelling enough, because the forms of religious life are frequently not thought through sufficiently in the light of the religious' function as teachers. Thus the vow of poverty may be lived with great austerity by religious in their individual rooms or their community room; but the spirit of poverty does not shine through either their way of thinking, or the way of managing the budget for the school. And so it can happen that the standards for admitting students may in practice be far removed from evangelical poverty, etc.

In another sense, those who are educated in progressive institutions see all too often only one aspect of the signs of God. They are deprived of the presence of those who witness to His transcendent love and to the eschatological realities of the faith. Thus one often notices that high school students in public schools easily confuse natural vitality with supernatural life, friendship with Christian love, natural desires with the will of God. The quality of their love or of their presence in the world is in danger of being ambiguous and of failing to proclaim the presence of God.

By oversimplifying somewhat, we might characterize these two tendencies as follows:

In religious institutions the signs are distorted primarily

through lack of fidelity to the values of the Incarnation: infidelity to the biblical language, to the historical impact of Jesus Christ, to the transforming power of His Resurrection.

In public schools, on the other hand, there is infidelity to transcendent values, so that the sign of the spiritual, eternal quality of God's presence in the world can hardly be recognized.

Were we to point out only negative factors, our diagnosis would risk being misleading, even unjust. Ultimately, it would be tantamount to saying that in effect Jesus Christ and the power of His Resurrection no longer exist. We would be offending the mercy of God.

The facts speak for themselves. Today as in ages past, the ceaseless action of the Holy Spirit calls forth signs; and we may even say that it calls forth signs which are singularly faithful to Jesus Christ and adapted to the needs of youth. We need only recall the different apostolic youth movements, Catholic Action, the religious renewal in many institutions and parish organizations. The vitality of the Church today does not lag behind that of previous centuries.

If they are to be touched in their hearts (we shall return to this later), young people must feel a youthful vigor in the signs of faith; they dislike pettiness, and delight in extremes. They need the closeness and warmth of friendship.

Despite the deficiencies we have mentioned, we must testify to the existence, even to the excellence, of such signs today. To mention only some: there is the growing number of young and dynamic priests who serve as chaplains of youth groups or in universities, and who bring to their young people sympathy and friendship. Nor should we forget the members of apostolic groups, the youthful quality of their work, the seriousness of their formation and of their thinking.[11]

The objective absence of the signs of faith from certain spheres of life in so-called Christian countries must give us pause. We have come a long way from the proclamations of the realities of the faith such as it existed during the Middle Ages—in the streets, the guild signs, the mystery plays, etc. —to the almost total silence of these same realities of Christ in our technological world.

Faced with this problem, let us first of all remember that the explicit proclamation of Jesus Christ depends on the Holy Spirit. His ways are mysterious and can accommodate themselves to an eclipse in some spheres, while becoming visible in others. We have been promised only one thing: that the Church will endure on earth "until the Lord returns." How or where this will happen we are not told. Will not the Church, which is the visible sign of the Lord, always be, materially speaking, "a little Church in the wide world,"[12] which represents and mysteriously draws together the great spheres of human life?

[11] We cannot give complete references here, from the press to the songs of P. Duval or of P. Bernard. We merely wish to emphasize that there are still signs today, expressed at times in very youthful, daring forms (which is not displeasing to the generation of Elvis Presley!). We need only recall the wave of generosity and enthusiasm stirred up by Abbé Pierre, the worker priests, the songs of P. Duval, etc.

[12] Yves Congar, O.P., The Wide World, My Parish (Baltimore: Helicon, 1961).

We should not be surprised at the astonishing ways in which the Gospel penetrates the world. The Spirit always breathes where He wills. All He asks of us is that we place our intellect at His service, so that human and divine initiative may meet in the proclamation of the signs of faith.

These thoughts should guide the impulse of our Christian charity. Faithful to Jesus Christ and to the purest tradition of the Church, we should feel the urge to plant the signs of faith in those places where, in the light of the Holy Spirit, they seem particularly urgently needed today: in the technological and scientific world—the world of the future; in the world of the worker[13]—the world of the "poor," whom the Lord loves with a special love.

These reflections should also lead us to examine, again and again, the manner in which we manifest and proclaim to the world the signs of faith in our own lives. Evangelical and missionary effectiveness is not a matter of numbers, nor of results that can be counted. What matters is above all the quality of the call and a spiritual leaven at the heart of the human mass. Do we still say today, when confronted with the signs of the Lord: "Will the Messiah, when He comes, work greater miracles than This Man?"

The problem for the conscience of Christians today is not so much that of adding up the number of conversions, but rather of making present the signs of Jesus Christ in the fullest possible truth. "And you, who do you say that I am?"

[13] This refers to the often destitute "working class" of France and other European countries. The term "worker" does not have the same meaning in the U.S.—Trans.

The Adolescent's Subjective Attitudes
Toward the Act of Faith

The subjective factors which dispose a man to commit himself to the Gospel can be summed up under three headings: 1) the sense of the sacred; 2) moral life; 3) the need for Redemption. Let us examine the ways in which the climate of our time, and adolescent psychology, either foster or hinder these subjective attitudes.

The sense of[14] the sacred is a reality which is hard to define and which takes on quite different forms depending on time and place. Fundamentally, it appears as the recognition by man of a meaning or power beyond his natural reach. Let us give some examples:

A young girl suddenly becomes aware of the presence of God in a beautiful landscape. Or: an adolescent is overwhelmed by the sense of a superior and transcendent force at the death of a friend. The religious meaning of a beautiful landscape, the sense of another world in the face of death—these are forces and meanings which overpower the young person. They irrupt into his vision of a familiar world, upsetting his balance. He is helpless before them, he feels as though he were the victim of a "beyond" which is stronger than he.

Thus the sense of the sacred appears as the subjective experience of the divine through a material mediation; as the encounter with a beyond which man cannot seize—a

[14] By *sense of* we understand a still implicit, vague knowledge in which intellect, affectivity, and will are involved but not yet differentiated. Cf. a "sense of humor," "business sense," etc.

vague reality which lacks a personal name (God the Father) and a precise, objective shape.[15]

It is important to note that the sacred is not an objective reality that can be clearly defined and distinguished from the profane. The "holy" that characterizes the great Soviet celebrations is not the same thing as the trembling and ecstatic "holy" of primitive dances. A careful analysis reveals that it is man who subjectively determines the holy, by associating objects, places or realities (such as death) with desires or meanings that are greater than he. It is also man who, according to his psychological makeup, environment or culture, colors the sense of the sacred in varying shades, either with a feeling of awe or of terror.

Generally speaking we can say that the sacred arouses a threefold reaction in man:

1) Fascination. Rudolf Otto speaks of fascination (fascinosum). The sacred does, indeed, appear to man at one and the same time as an instinctive need, and as infinitely beyond him. It draws and fascinates him, since it already exists potentially in his heart, as a call and a thirst, stamping his desires from the very first with the mark of the limitless and the absolute.

2) Fear and recoil. Otto also speaks of fear (tremendum). Confronted with forces which he cannot control and which escape his grasp, man says: "It had to happen," "Life's like that," "It's fate"—fatalistic phrases which express in reality a feeling of fear before the sacred. Magic is

[15] The classic work on the sacred is Rudolf Otto, The Holy. See also the writings of Mircea Eliade, especially: The Sacred and the Profane (New York: Harcourt, Brace, 1959).

nothing else than man's attempt to conciliate the Godhead
by forcing the mysterious and feared power to serve him.

3) Sense of the impossible. Because the "Absolute-
Transcendent" is beyond man, it is impossible for his intellect to grasp it. The sacred appears as something mysterious, something that his will cannot seize and subject to
itself.

Otto's study of the sacred among primitive peoples is enriched by the new insights which our times bring to his discoveries. The sense of the sacred represents, especially among
primitives, a becoming aware of a force "from beyond." "If
only the sky does not fall down on our heads," the ancient
Gauls used to say. This fear reveals the state of man at the
mercy of nature and of cosmic forces. All the sacred rites of
the past, writes P. Blanchet,[16] "humiliate man before the divine power and throw him into horror or ecstasy. Here the
human body has become a grimacing shell, which is manip-
ulated by the invisible fingers of the mystery; there, the
ecstasy grows and their eyes blaze." We have here a form of
the sacred which "falls upon" us, a sacred which separates
man from the "All-Other," a sacred of an absolute power;
in short, the sense of being crushed by one who is far
"above."

In the course of time certain natural phenomena have
little by little lost those mythical aspects which contributed
to a lesser degree to the sense of the sacred—such as fear of
a storm.[17] Man has also freed himself progressively from

[16] P. Blanchet, La littérature et le spirituel, I, 200.
[17] We need only recall the meaning which the Will o' the wisp in
the cemeteries held for medieval man.

the hold of a certain tragic sense of the sacred. Thus, the Romantics' sense of the sacred is already less frightening and overwhelming for man.

Thanks to the achievements of science man today tends to ban from the sacred everything that he cannot manipulate or control. Who knows but that he will hold in his hands before long the mastery of the forces of the universe, of history, and even of life itself? The earth is his, and he has no use for purposes and meanings which escape his scientific control. And so we may well ask whether the sense of the sacred will not disappear altogether before long.

By no means; but we must learn to recognize it in its new forms. The Church in her catechesis must take this new context into account.

Many people today experience the sense of the sacred not as a weight which falls upon them from above, but as a force which runs through history and matter. They have the sense of a superior force and meaning which are inherent in things, of an evolution toward a goal which is beyond the present. It appears less as the sense of the "All-Other from above," than as a beyond which is immanent to the movement of history.

It is interesting to note in this connection how Jean Jaurès[18] claims to find God through Marxist materialism:

Science, through the very progress of its discoveries and hypotheses on the origin of creatures and of life, has little by little dis-

[18] Jean Jaurès, *La question religieuse et le socialisme* (Paris: Editions de Minuit). No doubt, the idea of God in this book by Jaurès is a far cry from the traditional idea of the God of Christians; but we are here in the realm of the sacred.

pelled the prejudices against religion which it had at first created. For if living and conscious beings come into existence through a natural evolution inherent in the universe, this is so because the universe already contains in its depths consciousness and life. . . .

Evolution, therefore, which certain superficial people considered at first to be the death of religion, is on the contrary the experimental proof of God.

Furthermore, through this very doctrine of evolution, God is no longer a solitary abstraction. He is part of the movement and the life of the world. That ideal of beauty, of unity, and harmony which, according to Aristotle, fascinates the world and creates the different species by drawing them more or less closely to itself, does no longer act through a wholly metaphysical reality which is accessible to reason alone. It acts in time; it manifests itself in history.

Underlying this passage is a new expression of the sense of the sacred, which will flourish in all the attempts made by Marxists to evolve an eschatology of a limitless beyond of human freedom. We have here that new form of a Christian sense of the sacred which is apparent in the works of men like Lecomte de Noüy or Teilhard de Chardin.

Jaurès would say that if God seems to suffer an eclipse, it is because humanity must temporarily face up today to the demands posed by the conquest of nature, and must vehemently reject the forces of idealistic obscurantism. "Caught between the provocation of hunger and the excitement of hatred, humanity has no time to be concerned with the infinite. Mankind resembles a great tree swarming with angry flies beneath a stormy sky. In this humming of hatred the sonorous and divine voice of the universe can no longer be heard."

Another form of the sense of the sacred appears in the

frenzied pursuit of happiness, sunshine, subjective intoxication, of the exuberance of vitality and creative power.

Do not the great Chinese feasts, the Soviet observances,
the cult of the South Sea Islands, despite all their inherent
deviations conceal a longing for paradise? The sense of the
sacred manifests itself here as the sense of a "cosmic transcendence" of human plenitude, a "beyond" that escapes
man, and yet one which he cannot but dream of and desire,
just as one believes in a truth which is greater than oneself.

There are also those great questions which seize man in
the depth of his being—suffering and death. Modern man
remains sensitive to these realities as to the inevitable; but
it is not generally here that he experiences the sense of the
sacred. He tends rather to evade these problems, to thrust
them aside into the shadows or—as in the case of Marxism
—to smother them by a powerful will to create.

However great may be man's power today, the sense of
the sacred (or the religious sense) still survives in him, as
a fact which science can neither suppress nor avoid. Mayor
La Pira knew this very well when he said, speaking over
Radio Moscow, that men who are as serious, scientific and
positivist as the Russians, cannot refuse to recognize this
human reality.

If this is the situation of modern man in general, what
about the adolescent? Driven by his natural instincts which
are trying to assert themselves against an uncertain future,
placed in a nature which he has not yet learned to control,
the adolescent is more sensitive than the adult to the sacred,
especially to its ancient forms. Hero worship, the religious

symbolic sense, the need for an absolute, the thirst for justice to the point of rebellion, etc.—all these are marked characteristics of youth.[19] In the adolescent is verified the fact that the natural sense of the sacred is proportionate to man's biological drive. We find again here the idea of "the gods who are in one's blood."

This natural sense of the sacred is so strong in the adolescent that educators have exploited it. We need only recall certain speeches about idealism, or the prestige enjoyed by Antoine de Saint-Exupéry (Night Flight, and Wind, Sand and Stars), and the whole body of literature which came in its wake.

In recent years, however, the sense of the sacred has tended to be impaired, even among young people, by the impact of technological realism, of an all-pervasive materialism, and of "familiar naturalism."[20] The cult of idealism easily provokes smiles today and is superseded by the cult of human development which, at first sight, strikes a much less absolute note. The symbolic sense also seems less transparent today than it was in the 1940s.

Yet there can be no doubt that the sense of the sacred is particularly strong during adolescence and at the beginning of young adulthood, and that this constitutes its "sensitive

[19] Babin, op. cit., "Explication et synthèse."

[20] By familiar naturalism we mean a certain quality of modern life which results in a network of banal familiar contacts and of purely human intimacies. Modern life tends to suppress all search for grandeur. Advertising, radio, earthly cares keep man in a "familiar naturalism."

period."[21] The mysterious world of human love and the
reality of sex, which so easily upset the psychological balance
of young people, cannot fail to awaken in them resonances
that go beyond their confused and troubled emotions.

The sense of the sacred, then, is not the same at all stages
of life. In the presence of this "beyond" and "above" which
the death of a friend forces upon him, the adolescent does
not react in precisely the same way as the adult. Generally
speaking, the strongest elements in his sense of the sacred
will be a movement of fear or recoil, or of fascination with
the absolute, rather than a transcendent sense that is immanent in history, or the feeling of the impossible. He is also
more open to the divine meaning in things or events. He
"feels God," he "wants to reach the Ideal."[22] All these
reactions witness to his profound natural drives, as well as
to his insecure position in the world.

What is the relation between faith and the sense of the
sacred?

1) For a Christian, the sense of the sacred appears as a
natural phenomenon: man who is created by God retains
within himself the stamp of his Creator. The irresistible
desire for the absolute that haunts him is his birthmark.
The aspirations of his nature set in motion by his perception

[21] A term used by Maria Montessori. The absorbent mind does
not construct with a voluntary effort but according to certain "inner
sensitivities." These vary at different stages of man's life. The *sensitive period* lasts only for a definite time, until the acquisition due to
natural development has been achieved.

[22] We insist, in this notion of the sense of the sacred, on the sense
of purpose in the mysterious designs of a transcendent Being. The
sense of the sacred should not be reduced to a simple "force."

of the sacred are, however, only helpless appeals to the unknown God, whose face and designs of love are revealed to man by grace, in Jesus Christ.

This groping movement on the part of man remains nonetheless a subjective disposition for faith. By irrupting into man's innermost being, the sense of the sacred opens him to a world beyond himself, breaking down a first barrier of self-sufficiency. The anxiety and thirst for the infinite, the confused need—to the point of desperation—for boundless life which it arouses, all these constitute psychological prerequisites for the Beatitudes: "Blessed are the poor in spirit."

2) The sense of the sacred, however, is *not identical with faith*.[23] It is only a call, an implicit yearning for the Gospel. Many young people who have not been exposed to an enlightened catechesis will never go beyond vague stirrings of the spirit or nostalgic dreams. Disillusioned and perhaps embittered, the thirst for idealism is in danger of subsiding at the age of 25, when the instincts have become calm and the so-called realism of adulthood sets in.

3) We must note, finally, that the sense of the sacred has been *profoundly distorted by sin*. This was true among primitive peoples, who worshiped lightning or ancient trees. It is true today among scientists and technologists for

[23] "Christian faith inaugurates an entirely new relationship with God. Faith engulfs, in making it go beyond itself and purifying it, all that is superstitious and magical in religion. It has nothing to fear from the disappearance of certain superficial or childish forms of the sacred that are linked with a culture, with certain historical situations or psychological states. The time when the religious instinct grows less is often the very moment for a truly Christian faith and a more authentic sense of God." Liégé, *Adultes dans le Christ*, p. 23.

whom, at Los Alamos, the sense of the sacred has been
reduced to classified information on atomic energy. It is true
among young people, who say that they find life, "ecstasy
and God" in Rock 'n Roll.[24] We must insist that the perversion of the sense of the sacred tends, especially today, to
empty of its content the notion of transcendence. Modern
man tends to reject transcendence as a reality of another
world, and to put in its place a pseudo-transcendence which
is nothing but the limitless beyond of the world of man.

We can gain from all this some idea of the profound
ambiguity of the sense of the sacred, and of its need for purification. In many cases it has become so perverted that, instead of constituting an openness to faith, it is rather an
obstacle that subjects man to false gods—Rock 'n Roll, the
passion for sports, etc. It remains true, nevertheless, that the
sense of the sacred, the thirst for infinity, for the beyond, is
too natural to the adolescent to disappear completely. Catechesis will always find in it a point of support.

In summarizing, we can say that if the sense of the sacred
has not yet deserted the heart of modern man, rational, scientific culture tends to stifle the power of its call; and that,
furthermore, the idols of this world have insidiously har-
nessed its force to their advantage. Nothing essential has
been lost, but we must restore to the sense of the sacred its
proper role, which is to prepare the path for the God of
Jesus Christ.

At Jacob's well the Samaritan woman asked only for

[24] Cf. Jack Kerouac's book On the Road (New York: Viking,
1957), where the author deals with the Beat Generation's quest for
the absolute, for religion.

water to quench her thirst. Beginning with this natural
thirst, Christ knew how to arouse in her the thirst for living
water; and thus she came to know the gift of God.

With regard to the adolescent and moral life, we should
ponder these words of Jesus, "He who does the truth comes
to the light." He hereby defines succinctly the fundamental
condition of the act of faith and its law of growth.

"To do the truth" is a certain way of being, of deeply
committing all our resources at whatever stage we find
ourselves, to what we consider the truth. It is like a thread
woven into the tissue of one's choices, the "Thou shalt love
the Lord thy God with thy whole heart, and with thy whole
mind, and with thy whole strength." An upright and honest
life, genuine submission to the demands of the sacred and
of morality—all these make possible and foster growth in
faith.[25]

It is difficult to make a diagnosis of the moral life of adolescents, since much depends on individuals and on living
conditions. Let us simply point out that the adolescent has
the advantage of a powerful impetus of moral aspirations,
enthusiasm, and natural moral drives: a desire for Justice,

[25] In this context we should note an important study in *Information Catholiques Internationales* of April 1, 1960, on the mentality
of young people in the USSR. H. Peltier- Zamoiyska maintains that
moral preoccupations, which are very much alive among the Russians, bring them quite naturally to the question of transcendent
principles of morality. "Among young people, especially the more
sensitive ones, one finds at times a real agony, because they have
nothing to cling to. . . . The point of departure for a religious quest
is nearly always revolt of the conscience against injustice and lying"
(p. 30).

Truth, Brotherhood, Uprightness, Purity (all with capital letters). He seeks his own improvement and perfection, he likes a certain "asceticism."[26] All psychologists have remarked on the intensity and idealistic character of his moral aspirations. If we generally consider him today to be at the mercy of disordered and perverted instincts, we should also insist that he finds support in moral tendencies which are both strong and good.

In reference to his moral impetus we could define the adolescent as one who runs after the ideal image of himself with a maximum of Spartan intensity and idealism.[27]

What constitutes this ideal image of himself which he pursues? He tends first of all to make into an absolute man's natural tendencies—tendencies which could perhaps be supernaturalized, but which at this stage seem to be primarily natural because of the violence of the instincts. He tends to idealize his drives: "to lend a helping hand," etc.

He also makes an absolute of certain social demands which are deeply imbedded in his psychology and have become second nature to him. They are the product of education, of culture and his environment, and become crystal-

[26] Because of the ambiguous meaning of this word in English, "Spartan drive" might be more accurately used here.—Trans.

[27] This is proved by some lines from a teacher from one of the French provinces: "What is the aim of religion if not to fulfill the human being?" We might caricature this idea in the following schema:

| The ideal "ME" ⟵——— | religion, God, the others, sacraments seen as a means of self-realization |
| "ME"   ———⟶ | |

lized into formulas and simple slogans: "keep smiling," "be a good guy," etc.

Each milieu also has its own moral standards which the adolescent will tend to make into absolutes, whether it is a question of "friendship among peoples," of the "construction of the ideal democratic society," of the workers' welfare, or of the preoccupation with chastity in certain Christion circles. . . .

This ideal image is, finally, the projection into the absolute of certain character traits which have appeared in the course of his individual development. The adolescent likes himself and idealizes his character. Between 15 and 25 he will flaunt his individuality, whether it is vanity in dress, an unusual signature, or his crush on the latest movie idol.

This pursuit of the ideal self tends, as we have already remarked, to be carried on with great Spartan intensity and idealism. Adolescence constitutes a "sensitive period" for asceticism. In a book that has long been used as a manual in novitiates, Rodriguez[28] already made use of these psychological observations in setting up a ladder of perfection and inspiring young people with heroic examples.

In the world of sports as in the moral domain, the adolescent tends naïvely to exaggerate his own worth, to construct the sacred edifice of his ego.

Adolescents are often said to reject all law; it would be equally correct to say that they love the law. It is true that the young person rejects a law which seems to him to be imposed from without and to be unrelated to his person;

[28] *Practice of Perfection and Christian Virtues.*

but he cherishes those laws which appear to him necessary for his own success. This is proved by his Spartan drive, his love of methodical effort in attaining a goal. He is willing to put up with all sorts of hardships in order to develop himself.[29]

Such a sketch, which neither is, nor claims to be, a full portrait, but is rather a study of man's inclinations, once again reveals the fundamental ambiguity of his natural drives.

In the light of the Gospel we must clearly point out all that is dangerous in the moral aspirations of the adolescent. We might think a priori that the instinctive perversions of chastity and of love, and his crazy escapades, constitute the most serious dangers for the faith. The Gospel sees it otherwise.

In the eyes of Christ, the greatest danger is Pharisaism, that self-sufficiency which hardens the heart.[30] The publi-

[29] Simone de Beauvoir's efforts to "cultivate virtue" provide an extreme example of the Spartan drive: "I was much less interested in remote political and social questions than in the problems that concerned me personally: morality, my interior life, my relationship with God. . . . From year to year my piety became stronger, purer, and I came to despise morality in favor of mysticism. I prayed. I meditated. I tried to make the divine presence sensible to my heart. I sought out mortifications: shut up in closets which were my sole hiding place I scrubbed myself with a pumice stone until I was bleeding. I scourged myself with the golden chain I wore around my neck."—*Memoirs of a Dutiful Daughter* (Cleveland: World Publishing Co., 1959).

[30] Pharisaism sins in not recognizing the common lot of humankind: total dependence on God's mercy, freely given and not merited. Pharisaism "can essentially be described as the heresy of

cans occupy a higher rank in the Kingdom of God than the Pharisees.

It is easy to discover an analogy between the adolescent's desire for virtue and that of the Pharisee. Like the Pharisee the adolescent, in the grip of his natural tendencies, is in danger of constructing his perfection with his own hands. While the drive of his moral aspirations can help him "to do the truth and to come to the light," it can just as easily block the road, either through the deviations of egoistic enjoyment or—and still more surely—through Pharisaism. We must not trust too much in moral aspirations. We should even mistrust, with evangelical insight, a certain uprightness of life that is too organized and sure of itself. Jesus was recognized by Mary Magdalen rather than by the Pharisees.

The adolescent frequently feels a powerful need for redemption. "What really made me discover Christ," wrote a 16-year-old boy, "was my misery, the terrific need I had at one point to hold on to someone."

The humble recognition of our sinfulness and of evil in the world, the feeling of our inability to save ourselves— these constitute a sure access to faith. "I did not come for

religious autarchy or self-sufficiency, . . . as a way of living and an ideal for life. It is the unconscious but active conviction that in religious matters one must take his destiny into his own hands. And this means nothing less than that one can determine one's own eternal fortune, as also the unique meaning and tenor of one's entire life. This is really the essence of pride, as illustrated by Luke, chapter 18." W. K. Grossouw, *Spirituality of the New Testament* (St. Louis: B. Herder, 1961), p. 90.—Trans.

the healthy, but for the sick and for sinners." Recognition of our condition as sinners is basic to the act of faith. It is striking to see that, whenever young people around the age of 20 go through the crisis of conversion, their openness to God nearly always goes hand in hand with a recognition of their pride, vanity, and selfishness. A young girl of 22, during a conversation which had been preceded by many others seemingly without result, suddenly stopped arguing and, with tears in her eyes, threw aside her mask of self-sufficiency: "I am proud, I have loved only myself until now, I tried to make others serve me. It's awful!" Soon afterward she asked to go to confession.

It is above all at the moment of reaching the last stage of adolescence that the young person is sensitive to the experience of failure. The adolescent sets out on the road of life full of illusions and sure of success. The adult, already "scorched" by experience, has managed to surround himself with a network of security; but the adolescent, not yet on firm ground but already emerging from the boundless dreams of his 15 years, comes up against failure: failure of his ideas, his dreams and aspirations, the experience of an inhuman world, a burning awareness of his own moral weakness and sinfulness.

This is indeed an important and dangerous moment, since it can lead just as easily to proud rebellion as to humble admission of his weakness. The experience of failure and of sin can produce either a Nietzsche or a Mary Magdalen. If they find spiritual help at this critical stage, many young people will begin to face the fact that they are sinners. This will be decisive for the act of mature conversion some years later.[31]

If this humble recognition of his personal sin and of the sin of the world is not an isolated act, but is repeated with every new disappointment and failure, the young person's faith in Christ the Saviour will deepen and grow. If, on the other hand, failure hardens him or throws him back into disillusionment and bitterness, the attitudes of simplicity and poverty, so essential for the Beatitudes, will be impaired. With some, purely natural and proud rationalizations will now gain the upper hand: they will challenge God, they will blame Him for evil as though they were greater than He.

The failure of the adolescent's vitality is therefore an essentially ambiguous experience, a key that can either open or shut the door to God's coming. It should be stressed that at this critical point the influence of a Christian, or of the teacher, can be decisive. If at this very moment the adolescent knows that he can count on a disinterested person, he will swallow punishment. It is less difficult to accept yourself as weak and little and to believe in the signs of God if you discover in a human face close by that there is someone who takes you seriously and insists on trusting you.

[31] A young man told us: "What made me lose the faith was my idealism. I believed too much in the ideal. I ran after it but I couldn't reach it. Then I let go of everything." This boy had identified Christianity with natural idealism. Instead of accepting the salvation brought by Christ he despaired of an illusory ideal, which was nothing but a projection of something beyond himself.

Fundamental Ambiguity of the Adolescent

The stage of adolescence as such is fundamentally ambiguous. It is both a chance and a danger for the subjective attitudes to the signs of faith. We have tried to show that the power of his sense of the sacred, of his moral sense, or of sense of failure, can either foster or harm the adolescent's commitment, and lead either to a deepening of faith or to its rejection.

Let us make two comments by way of conclusion:

1) The adolescent's biological drive will strengthen his subjective disposition toward faith. Strong vital drives force his to throw off his torpor or his childhood supports and propel him, at times dramatically, into taking a clear-cut position. Thus conditioned by his age he will be obliged to ask himself questions and to seek personal solutions. His subjective attitudes will naturally be hot or cold, rather than lukewarm.[32]

[32] In an interview on her book, *Aimez-vous Brahms*, Françoise Sagan expressed the importance of youth as the age in which religious and metaphysical questions are asked:
"What is the meaning of your title, *Aimez-vous Brahms?*"
"It sums up the entire book for me. A woman of 40 is suddenly asked: 'Aimez-vous Brahms?' (Do you love Brahms?). This is a question you put to someone at the age of 20, it is a question you put to a young person."
"What sort of questions does one ask at 20? And later?"
"At 20 one asks: 'Do you believe in God?' 'Do you like Nietzsche or Brahms?' These questions have nothing to do with your private and daily life. Later you no longer ask such questions, you forget them as you grow older. Later one asks: 'Have you seen such and such a film?' 'Are you having an affair with So-and-So?' . . ."

2) Furthermore, the adolescent's instinctual drives and natural desires are so pervasive that their advantages are off-set by a risk: he is in great danger of falling prey to his sub-jectivity and sense-experiences. Thus he becomes almost in-capable of recognizing the objective signs of faith. When a boy of 15 is in love, his subjective feeling overwhelms him to the point that he no longer sees and loves the young girl for herself. So too the adolescent, imprisoned by his experi-ence of the God of nature, risks becoming insensitive or closed to the God of Revelation.

Along with Pharisaism, this danger of "immanence" seems to us to be the principal threat to faith during ado-lescence. As our study has shown, the natural craving to feel, to understand and to have something to lean upon risks being satisfied with a ready-made God who answers one's instinctive needs. Where this is so we are far from faith in the God of Revelation, which is humble recognition and firm cleaving to objective signs.[33]

The great task that confronts the religious education of adolescents would seem to be this: we must help them make the transition from a natural religion, or vague piety, to the religion of Jesus Christ; from a voluntarist attraction toward an ideal, to the fidelity of response to their personal calling.

The educator who has learned to see with the eyes of Christ will come to realize that the true Christian wealth of adolescence depends on him. It is up to him to recognize the helpless calls for true life expressed in frenzied dancing, and the implicit longing for the Kingdom of God which so

[33] Cf. Liégé, op. cit., pp. 22–23.

many current songs and jazz rhythms sing. The unchaining of the instincts so characteristic of adolescence is at least a hollowness which cries out to be filled. It is up to the teacher to reveal, to call, to arouse true life, by denouncing false happiness. In the face of excitements, of false ecstasies of dance, of failures, and of romantic dreams, the catechist must continue to prophesy about the "dry bones" so that they may come back to life.

Jesus, who knew the power of the Resurrection, did not take death seriously. In and through us, He says to the adolescent again and again: "Young man, arise."

CHAPTER TWO

THE CONVERSION OF YOUTH

Conversion: meaning and importance
in human development

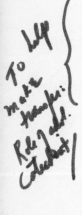

"I don't believe in a faith which has never been tried,"
writes E. Joly. "Whether we have grown up as a Catholic or
whether we have always lived in an atheistic environment,
sooner or later we must be converted to Jesus Christ. . . .
The normal age at which this happens is between 18 and
25."[1]

Emmanuel Mounier insists on the same point. Recalling a
retreat made at 20 he writes: "If we are worth anything at
all, we still have to undergo one or several conversions. The
transition from a traditionalist and bourgeois piety to a
genuinely Christian life—that is to say, to the life of humility and of charity—is at least as painful as the transition
from atheism to faith."

Some authors use words like "conversion," "transition,"
or "definite crisis" (according to E. D. Starbuck) in describ-

[1] E. Joly, *What Is Faith?* (New York: Hawthorne, 1958).

ing this critical moment. We must analyze it carefully.[2] For if man's life depends on two or three Yes's and No's, the Yes or No he speaks in this hour will profoundly mark the rest of his life. This hour of decision does not occur as a chance event, as a deus ex machina, but comes at the end of a slow process of maturing that is made up of much groping, reflection, and effort, and of all sorts of failures as well—like a fruit that falls from the tree after a long history of rain, wind, sunshine and night.

In the inner maturing of the life of faith this stage of conversion will have a sequel and completion. The conversion of youth is not yet the full maturity of faith. Nor is lapse from the faith at this time necessarily an irrevocable step that cannot be repaired. "There will be other Himalayas in the life of man." And yet, this moment is decisive in man's growth. For it marks a stage of his quest and a solidification of his personality. At a later time the young adult will make this choice more realistically and will ratify it in his mature confrontation with life.

Crises may be explicit and implicit. In the life of a person who is developing normally toward adulthood there is always a choice to be made, a taking of positions, which will stamp and give direction to his life. H. Godin, in *France Pagan*, stresses this in relation to young people who, around the age of 18–20, pass through a crisis of reflection and

[2] P. Babin, "La foi au terme de l'adolescence en milieu scolaire," in The proceedings of the Second National Congress of Religious Education, Paris 1957, pp. 171 ff. (Sections of this article appeared in the *Grail Bulletin of Religious Education, No. 13*, and were reprinted in *Religious Education, March–April* 1962.—Trans.)

idealism. For many of them the choice of a profession or
job, of a political, social or religious commitment, or of marriage, make this moment decisive. A young girl put it this
way: "In accepting his love I feel that I am committing my
whole life, and my fidelity to Christ; no one has the right to
interfere with my freedom."

The choice may also, however, be implicit; taking a stand
may be more or less conscious and voluntary. Some are
satisfied with simply ratifying a situation in which they find
themselves. Far from always appearing as a dramatic crisis,
conversion (or lapse from the faith) takes more commonly
the form of a subtle, gradual development.

The D-Day of "conversion-commitment" is often preceded by lesser crises or by small failures in the life of faith.
Such are those sudden changes that are typical of adolescence, especially between 15 and 20, and which make the
young person choose temporarily a certain form of life or
commitment. These peaks and valleys do not have an absolute meaning in themselves; they prepare the way for tomorrow's commitment and for the hour when the decisive
choice will be made. Since childhood and adolescence culminate in this moment, which is the climax of youth, it is
necessary to study more closely the different types and
characteristics of conversion (or lapse from the faith), before we describe the stages of maturing in faith.

We can distinguish[3] three main types of conversion: 1)

[3] This study is based on a number of concrete cases. The second
part of Simone de Beauvoir's *Memoirs of a Dutiful Daughter* seems
to us to be typical of a certain kind of rejection of the faith. We
shall refer to this book more than once.

explicit conversion (or lapse); 2) implicit conversion (or lapse); 3) conversion (or lapse) through ratification of a given situation.

Explicit Conversion or Lapse from the Faith

Certain people with a more reflective or introspective bent of mind, who are particularly sensitive to the influences of the world and to their own subjective drives, suffer a violent crisis of faith between the age of 15 and 25. Some of them admit that they have lived in such grave doubt and religious anxiety that they could no longer sleep.

A young man of 18 writes: "Before making up my mind I spent a whole night without being able to sleep." E. Renan compared his crisis "to an inflammation of the brain, during which all other life-functions were suspended."[4] Finally, at the height of the crisis, one's whole being gathers its forces, tautens, and surrenders itself in an act of humble faith; or, on the contrary, rises in an act of refusal and concludes that God does not exist. "I realized that God no longer intervened in my life, so I concluded that He had ceased to exist for me" (Simone de Beauvoir).

This act involves man's entire being and remains deeply engraved in his memory. Describing such a moment a young man of 21 writes: "It happened quietly, in a small chapel, one morning that I shall never forget. I was all alone. . . ." And a young girl: "It was during confession, after a last, stormy interview with a priest, in a large room . . ."

[4] E. Renan, *Souvenirs d'enfance et de jeunesse*, p. 220.

Wherein does this decisive act of faith or conversion of youth consist? From a purely psychological viewpoint we could define it as the act or event in which the young person gives his life a direction and meaning in relation to transcendent values, with a depth of consciousness and decision that put an end to the vacillations of his adolescence and profoundly affect the moral and religious sense of his adult life.[5]

In its Christian form we could define it as an act through which the young person, having recognized his insufficiency and sinfulness, chooses, in a moment of intense consciousness, Jesus Christ as the meaning of his life, and more particularly as the solution to his thirst for "amounting to something," for improving himself, and for intellectual security.[6]

The characteristics of the conversion of youth are:

1) *The desire for happiness seems to be more important*

[5] We say profoundly, not definitively, for this act is still subject to revision. Sometimes the definitive aspect of taking a moral and religious stand during youth will become apparent only later, in adulthood. By that time (35–40) man has, as it were, entrenched himself in his situation, made himself prisoner of his history, and has attained a certain synthesis of thought and values.—Cf. an interview with Françoise Sagan at the age of 24: "24 is not the same as 20. When I was 19 I could be completely changed by someone, or discover something through another person. Now I no longer believe in this sort of thing. I can change my life, be happy or unhappy, but I can no longer change a succession of reflexes that are myself. I can be changed only through myself."

[6] Such a conversion appears to be quite anthropocentric. Let us remember that we have here a psychological analysis at a given age. Mature Christian conversion will contain more objective, sacrificial elements.

psychologically than the desire for truth. In choosing Jesus Christ as the meaning of his life, he commits himself totally: "Faith is the act of a person who unites himself to another person." In the concrete unity of this step, "love is the gateway to faith, . . . love penetrates and directs knowledge."[7]

And yet, in this total commitment of faith the interplay of the intellect and will does not seem to be the same at every stage of life. "The act of faith," says St. Thomas, "is an act of the intellect determined partly by the power of the will. Thus it is related to the object of the will, which is the good, and to the object of the intellect, which is the true."[8]

In the adolescent's act of conversion it is above all the attraction of the *good*, of the end (object of the will) which is the starting point, rather than the attraction of the *true* (object of the intellect). It is his desire to be happy, to succeed in life, to be done with his metaphysical fears and anxiety, that are the preponderant motives for his faith. Although his desire for happiness includes a desire for truth as well, the latter does not at this stage manifest all the demands which it will make later.

The need for objective guarantees of faith does no doubt exist, and these guarantees have often been carefully studied; but what drives the adolescent to conversion is the urge to escape from a hopeless situation, the desire to be a success in life, rather than the challenge of objective truth. In his

[7] Mouroux, *I Believe*, p. 43.
[8] II–II, q. 2, art. 2.

conversion he gives himself to God because God is "his good," rather than because God is true.

It would be a mistake, theoretically and psychologically, to separate the two aspects; but we must emphasize the main motivations of his act of faith. The faith of the adult, on the other hand, is more sensitive to the element of objective truth.[9]

2) *Undifferentiated knowledge.* Without delaying over individual details of Revelation, the adolescent believes above all "in God," "in religion," "in Jesus Christ,"[10] phrases that reveal the preponderance in his faith of trust and surrender of his whole being.

This aspect appears to be complementary to the preceding one. We have seen that, at the basis of the adolescent's act of faith, there is a craving for happiness, or (this amounts to the same thing), for personal development. Development, for him, is first of all making secure the foundations of the life that is opening up before him,

[9] This is important for the catechetical presentation. Without separating the true from the good our catechesis should nevertheless stress life and happiness, as Jesus did in the Gospel. St. Thomas himself writes: "Since the chief object of faith consists in those things which we hope to see, according to Hebrews 9:1—'Faith is the substance of things hoped for'—it follows that those things are in themselves of faith which order us directly to eternal life"— II–II, q. 1, art. 6, ad 1.

[10] This does not contradict the nature of the act of faith; quite to the contrary. St. Thomas writes (II–II, q. 11, art. 1): "Whoever believes, assents to someone's words. Therefore, in every form of belief, the person to whose words assent is given seems to hold the chief place and to be the end as it were; while the things . . . hold a secondary place. Consequently, he that holds the Christian faith aright, assents, by his will, to Christ. . . ."

clinging to a reality which is greater than he and which will give him security on his road into the future. God, for him, is simply the reality to whom he entrusts himself.

We must not exaggerate the personal character of his relationship with God. The adolescent is still too idealistic; he conceives God naïvely as the "absolute Reality" who has all the answers to his questions, and hardly sees Him as a Person who has revealed Himself historically. St. Thomas uses the following phrase, which is inspired by St. Augustine: "Faith is to believe God, to believe that God exists, to believe in God." It is the third aspect that matters most to the adolescent.

We must again stress here the importance of the will in this "believing in God": "If the object of faith is considered in so far as the intellect is moved by the will, an act of faith is *to believe in God*. For the First Truth is referred to the will, through having the aspect of an end."[11]

3) *The act of conversion involves a new vision of reality and a moral decision.* In contrast to lapse from the faith, conversion directly involves on the adolescent's part a personal recognition of his sinfulness and a humble decision to change his life. It was at the very moment when the Samaritan woman accepted Christ's awareness of her moral condition ("You have had five husbands") that she recognized Him as Messiah.

In accepting Christ the young person agrees at the same time to have his self-sufficiency and egoism denounced. This will be more or less marked, depending on the individual;

[11] II–II, q. 11, art. 2.

but there can be no doubt that every conversion involves a decision to change morally, and a new way of looking at reality, at life, at the commitments and choices that must be made.

4) *The act of conversion stamps decisively the direction of life.* Because the conversion of youth takes place at the end of a gradual development which frees the personality from its childhood supports and the caprices of a vacillating adolescence, it seriously commits one's life and quickly becomes crystallized in the choice of a profession, vocation, or marriage.

The explicit lapse from the faith will by analogy have the same characteristics as conversion: desire for happiness, rather than for truth.

Simone de Beauvoir describes her rejection of God as follows: "I plunged my hands into the cool cherry-laurel, I listened to the splashing of the water, and I understood that nothing could induce me to give up the joys of this earth. 'I no longer believe in God,' I told myself with surprise."

A young girl of 18 writes in a similar vein: "I love the human for the sake of the human, and men for the sake of men. Religion no longer satisfies me. God, such as he has been shown to me, does not satisfy me. He does not answer all the needs of my soul. I don't think that I have found the truth; but the truth which I thought I had found is incompatible with my being. It seems unnatural to me. . . ."

Instead of moral conversion we have here moral deviation. Faith gives us a new vision of reality to which we conform our life. Rejection of the faith also gives us a new vision of reality; but the moral deviation often leads to a perversion that may be defined in these words: "Whatever suits me is true and good." The very notion of truth is here distorted. "The truth which I thought I had found is *incompatible with my being*, it seems unnatural to me." In the words of Jean Cocteau, "You do not tell a lie; you have become a lie."[12]

Implicit Conversion or Lapse

For one reason or another the majority of people do not experience a violent crisis of faith. This may be due to weak personal vitality,[13] or to a stunted development or education, or—more frequently—to the fact that the circumstances of their daily life do not force them to make a choice.

Many young people, who live in a pagan environment in which the Gospel is not preached, pose to themselves the question of conversion only in implicit terms of natural religion or of local moral standards. Their crisis of faith will be less severe.[14]

[12] Today especially we see the appearance, under the pressure of materialism, of a type of moral deviation which makes subjective development the norm of freedom and morality. It is the "I" which makes God of itself. Truth, like morality, is whatever fits in with my personal development (cf. below, pp. 122 ff.). Jesus Christ, because of His objectivity, is totally rejected.

[13] Either because they are not particularly sensitive to the main currents of the outside world, or because weak instincts spare them interior turmoil.

[14] This is the case of all those who are saved through *implicit* adherence to the Church.

Many others, on the contrary, who live in Christian structures hardly touched by the standards of the pagan world, will quite naturally make the transition from the security of a childhood faith to a faith set in a sociological context that is Christian. The enticement of the pagan world hardly reaches them, and the attractiveness of Christian values will save them from a dramatic crisis.[15]

Others, finally, are preoccupied with immediate, concrete problems, such as work or marriage, that make greater depth and consistent reflection impossible.

We should not conclude that this vast number of young people will not grow in faith, or that they are incapable of reaching spiritual maturity. The implicit nature of their conversion may, however, produce a weaker Christian vitality.

Implicit conversion is painted essentially in the same colors as explicit conversion, but in lighter hues: the intellect and, above all, the will play a less prominent role. Whereas in the explicit conversion the problem of faith is confronted as such, rather vaguely connected with questions of social involvement, vocation, or profession, in the implicit conversion the latter predominate and lead eventually to a Christian way of life.

The problem which faces the young person here is not directly God in Himself. Rather, it is the concrete involvement in a form of action or of life which commits him to

[15] Many French Canadians, Spaniards, Italians, or even some Frenchmen have told us that this was their case: the allurement of wordly prestige was practically nonexistent for them. We would also include here all those who live in a social environment that is sure of itself, safe, and gives man confidence in himself and his future.

some definite position. By refusing to get involved in this apostolic movement or that friendship, or in a team, he actually dodges the issue of conversion. This will sooner or later result in a more decisive refusal to live his faith.

In the implicit conversion there is less of a taking of sides concerning the object of faith in its conceptual form; the adolescent's attitudes will be determined by certain people, structures, and concrete commitments.[16] At the time of marriage, or when he commits himself to a political or religious cause—in other words, when he settles down to his particular way of life—the young person will also settle down to his own view of Christianity.

Generally speaking the implicit conversion, which we would prefer to call here Christian commitment, has the following characteristics: 1) Wholesale allegiance to a creed and morality, out of loyalty to the Church. This creed and morality are never questioned, but take forms that are often vague and are expressed in formulas and slogans: "God takes care of us," "love is everything," "marriage is for life," etc. 2) Adherence to certain ways of doing things, to certain religious practices (Sunday Mass, etc.). 3) Adherence to certain structures, people,[17] forms of action. 4) Adherence

[16] It would be wrong to deny that, at a given moment, these young people make certain moral or philosophical reflections; but generally speaking these are not solved on the level of reason. Nor do they have that urgency which we find in people of a more intellectual type.

[17] "We often become converted to a person at least as much as to the Church." Cf. the importance of the pastor in certain parishes. Or, the case of a dying man who asks for the priest and tells him: "It was V. B. who made me do it. If a man like him wanted to receive the last sacraments, so do I."

to certain deep-seated principles of loyalty, will, generosity, of sacrifice, charity, etc.

It will depend on the adolescents themselves, as well as on their teachers, whether such a conversion will deepen and bear rich fruit for their spiritual life, or whether it will remain that good seed "fallen among the thorns" which never reaches maturity.

Briefly, then, this implicit conversion is characterized by its relation to concrete facts, actions, and commitments, and by its lack of interiority, reflection and, most of the time, of intellectual awareness. Many people have neither the means nor the time of possibility to come to a conceptual systematization of their faith.[18] Many, moreover, especially in so-called Christian countries, face neither subjective religious problems nor interior difficulties. Their Christianity is as much a part of them as their breathing, and they are not forced from the outside to a definite choice. Growth in faith and in its conceptualization happens automatically for

[18] This has serious consequences for the education of faith. We must indeed aim at intellectualizing the faith, as a more perfectly human form of commitment in faith. But we may not lose sight of that vast crowd who will never make the commitment of faith except through gestures, emotional involvement, prayer and formulas. The Church's liturgy and life of charity can show us the way.—We have here also one of the basic lines that religious education should take in technical schools. It seems that these young people are not open to abstract thought, but that it is indeed possible to reach them through Christian gestures, facts, images, clear formulas, and above all through concrete religious commitments. Is not this what the *Reader's Digest* does on another level when it "educates" human development with stories like: "The most unforgettable character I ever met," "The best advice I ever received," etc.?

them, quite objectively and gently. And yet they too will reach a moment of conversion; but perhaps through falling in love, or choosing a vocation or way of life.[19]

We can thus distinguish two kinds of implicit conversion:

1) Implicit conversion *without adequate reflection* and intellectual awareness. This is the case among adolescents who are in touch with the world but who have no opportunity to deepen their knowledge of the faith. They may take a strong vital stand, but their intellectual grasp will be weak.

2) Implicit conversion *without a vital and deliberate decision*. Here the intellectual and especially the abstract knowledge may be great, but the struggle and decision for faith are weak. This is the case among those whose capacity for making free decisions is less developed, or who live in a sheltered environment.

We shall find the same characteristics in the implicit lapse from the faith as in the implicit conversion; not a theoretical taking of sides, but rather the rejection of certain religious practices—attitudes which will all too readily be accompanied by criticism of individual priests or of the Church as a whole. It is not God in Himself who is rejected here but the concrete fact which speaks of God—the Church, Christians, the priesthood. "I believe in God, of course, but not in priests. Look what Father X did, . . ." etc.

[19] It is obvious that in this perspective our catechesis will need to be less closely "related." In such sheltered environments adolescents are often said to have no serious problems of faith; it is enough to continue to surround them with strong, objective structures. This is partly true. Nevertheless, we must awaken in them a personal viewpoint, arouse questions, and take as our starting point, not theoretical problems of faith that don't exist, but concrete questions of vocation, profession, love, moral development.

Often such an attitude is due to the influence of bad friends or a harmful atmosphere.

Conversion (or Lapse) Through the Ratification of a Given Situation

Many people who are driven by particular circumstances, or who lack psychological maturity, have committed themselves without sufficient awareness to certain situations in which they find themselves one day imprisoned. For instance: a girl wants to get away from her domineering mother and marries the first man who comes along; or, a young man in financial straits enters a profession he dislikes.

How many young men or women thus find themselves one day definitively involved in a situation which they had not clearly enough foreseen! At the same time, the religious dimension of their involvement was hardly willed or considered consciously; it was determined chiefly by circumstances or the force of childhood habits. They practice their religion because their parents considered it the thing to do (childhood habit); or, they no longer go to Mass because their marriage partner has decided that he won't go (circumstances, sociological factors).[20]

In such cases, generally speaking, either a lack of maturity or the demands of a situation that must subsequently be faced (e.g., a profession or marriage) stifle subjective drives

[20] We find here frequent cases of people who have already undergone an "implicit conversion" in a Christian milieu, but who are so severely shaken by a sudden change in their circumstances that the whole world of faith is suddenly questioned, e.g., the shocks produced by a change of school, military service, or emigration.

and religious anxiety. The crisis of faith, therefore, may be considerably delayed or drag on inarticulately for a long time.

Whereas strong subjective needs or worries lead to taking a stand on religious matters in the explicit conversion, we find in the conversion "by ratification" that it is usually failure in a given situation that will provoke serious religious questioning. For instance: a woman of 25, baptized, married outside the Church, runs away from home because of her husband's brutality. After some deliberation she agrees to go back to him, but on condition that their marriage be ratified by the Church and that they change their way of life. It was failure which, in this instance, crystallized the crisis of conversion.

To put it more simply: there are many people who, between 25 and 40, find themselves suddenly involved in a situation which they had not clearly foreseen or willed. The suffering which they now experience brings them face to face with religion and the will of God. Some will harden themselves and rebel. They will get a divorce, refusing perhaps to forgive those who had driven them against the wall. Others will avoid the problem by running away from it. Instead of getting a divorce they will seek refuge in amusement or will throw themselves into feverish, meaningless activities, refusing to face up to their situation. Others, finally, will ratify their situation in the light of faith.

The ratification of a given situation in faith (marriage, profession, sickness, environment) can be for many people a very high form of the conversion of youth. For example, a young girl who is engaged is stricken by polio. After a moment of crisis and rebellion she recognizes "the passage of the Lord" in her life and wholeheartedly surrenders to His will. She attains great sanctity, peace, and joy.

We find here once again all the elements of the explicit conversion, especially the recognition of the concrete and personal signs of God in one's life.

It was important for us to analyze at some length this point of arrival which is the heart of conversion and toward which the adolescent's whole life of faith is pointing. For we may never forget that all the turmoil, efforts, and upheavals which affect his spiritual life must be understood and interpreted not in themselves, but in relation to their goal.

From a psychological viewpoint we may say that the conversion of youth is the vantage point against which his whole religious crisis is to be understood. God wills this conversion, which is so eminently personal. When it is a matter of man's freedom, God fears neither battles nor agonies, nor even the dangers of rejection.

It will now be relatively easy for us to perceive the direction in which the adolescent's life of faith will develop in order gradually to reach maturity. We shall see that the difficulties and degrees of maturing in faith correspond to the psychological stages of adolescence.

CHAPTER THREE

STAGES IN THE GROWTH OF FAITH

The aim of this chapter is to describe the maturing of faith in adolescence. In order to situate this age in its proper context, however, we shall first consider childhood and then briefly indicate the main lines that lead toward adulthood.

Adolescence is a period of profound changes. Hence it involves struggles and crises which will eventually resolve themselves in a new equilibrium. As the young person comes face to face with life he must fight his way forward. It will be our task here to describe this laborious passage, to measure its risks and dangers, and the possibilities of going astray.

The observer is first of all struck by a negative aspect. When the child who is learning to swim leaves the solid land for the first time, he feels lost, with nothing to hold on to. Will he drown? His swimming teacher who watches his pupil's efforts to stay afloat does not give way to panic. Neither should the educator let himself be unnerved by the risks and mistakes of adolescence, for these are only the reverse side of positive values. God wills these risks. Through them He calls the adolescent to the apprenticeship of his freedom. Only at this price will he truly become a son of the Kingdom.

This is our perspective. In the light of faith we shall try to adopt God's positive view of the adolescent. And if the deviations that may occur frighten us, let us not forget Christ's way of seeing them. Our vision is informed by that of the Risen Lord, the Christ whom we know to be capable of taking to Himself and saving man in all his terrestrial dimensions—adolescence as well as adulthood.

The Beginnings of the Life of Faith: Childhood

In analyzing the act of faith we insisted above all on its personal aspect, so that we could discern clearly the role of the individual. We must not, however, lose sight of its communal, social, and ecclesial character. Faith is an act of the Church, by which the Church on earth begins, here and now, to see reality according to the vision of the Church in heaven.

The act of faith is always a communal act, within the Church, supported and "made" by the whole Church. The extent to which this is so can be seen particularly clearly in the case of the child. For the less differentiated and developed a person's freedom, the more does his life of faith appear to be carried by the Church.[1] The infant is literally "inserted" into the faith by the instrumentality of those

---

[1] This is the case for the infant before the age of reason; for mentally retarded children; for the sick person whose faculties are impaired; and in general for all forms of infantilism which are due to a faulty education, or to sociological structures so strong that they have hindered the individual's normal development.

around him: the Church's part in his baptism, his parents'
love ... These "mediations" allow God's operative presence
to reach him.

F. L. Guittard speaks at this age of an "imitative faith."
The phrase can be retained, provided the meaning of the
word "imitation" includes identification and osmosis. The
infant may be compared to a sponge which is born in the
ocean and nourished by its waters and which, as it grows
and becomes differentiated, absorbs more and more actively
the lifegiving waters that surround it.

Thus the child will bring to his growth in faith an ever
more active and personal part, as his faculties awaken. Born
of the Church, he continues to draw his life from her. Far
from severing him from the community that has carried
him, his increasingly personal living will root him more
solidly within her. He is not to invent some sort of
Credo of his own, but to participate more actively, consciously and freely, in the faith of the Church—just like the
sponge that achieves full growth, not by leaving the waters
of the ocean but by being immersed in them more and
more fully.

Let us first note the importance of the influences in the
subconscious levels of his being which condition the child's
piety from his very first moments. The vital relationship
which the infant forms with his parents conditions[2] his own
relationship with the transcendent God, the heavenly
Father.

[2] Cf. the thesis of Bovet (Pestalozzi). In contrast to psychoanalysis, we speak here only of conditioning: faith and the sense of
God are not the result of our relationship with our parents.

Through the feeling of grandeur, of strength and power which his father's love awakens in the child's heart, the father is instrumental in calling forth in him the sense of a God who is great and transcendent. The mother, on the other hand, through her goodness, her selfless love and affectionate presence, awakens in her child's heart a sense of the love of God, of His presence, of being "safe" with Him. In the case of Christian parents we may rightly speak here of a certain precatechesis in the broad sense, through "empathy." Hence it is important that parents, who are the primary educators of their children, resemble as much as much as possible the heavenly Father: goodness and strength, attentive presence, selflessness. We find here the two elements that are necessary for a proper balance—spontaneity and authority.[3]

The religious education of children who were deprived of such an atmosphere in their first years often faces many obstacles. These children are full of complexes. "I can't believe that God, or anyone else, loves me," said a girl of 20 who had been abandoned by her parents. "No one has ever loved me." She had never in her life experienced the joy of being loved; the conditioning of her early years had been at fault.

This lack of love from which so many people of our generation suffer is the cause of that loneliness, that "neurosis of anxiety which is the sickness of the capitalist

[3] Cf. Fritz Künkel, *The Psychotherapy of Character*, as well as Künkel's whole theory of character-types. He analyzes with great insight the concrete operation of the subject's élan in confronting authority and deduces from it all the consequences for the subjective appreciation of values.

world,"[4] of that compensation by feverish activity and domination which lead to a subjective feeling of the absence of God.

We should also stress the importance during early childhood of coming to the age of reason, which is marked by the awakening of spiritual liberty and responsibility. If we insist too much at this time on a morality of obedience or on punishment, we may kill the child's spontaneity. Already at this early age a delicate formation of conscience is called for, one in which authority and obedience, law and spontaneity, will be wisely blended.

We must be guided by the true notion of authority as revealed in the Bible: an authority which "allies" itself with the child's drives and enters into dialogue with his aspirations, in an authentic climate of God's Covenant with man.

The period from 9 to 12 is more objective, realistic, practical and active, as well as more "social" (less subjective and introverted). The instinctual drives are less strong. The child is now ready for a broader, more systematic catechesis, in which memory and objective understanding play a greater role. He is also ready at this time for a more ordered Christian life, molded by good habits and even by a certain amount of conformism.

The danger at this time is that the child will "put on" religious teaching, the influence of the school and parish, like clothing that is unrelated to his inner life. Hence the risk of individualism and of a compartmentalization of life.

[4] Cf. the thesis of Karen Horney, in *The Neurotic Personality of Our Time* (New York: W. W. Norton, 1937). Also the studies of Gertrude von le Fort.

On the one side there is religion—doing religious things "I am told to do," "being good"; on the other there is life—playing, fighting, getting ahead in school.

Educators should not be deceived by the facile, illusory success of their authority and prestige. They should help the child to go beyond a religion and morality of obedience. A mold can turn out individuals; but it is love, the call to the heart, which awakens free human beings.

Along with a piety that is more social and objective, we should also awaken in him the sense of living relationships and of listening to the voice of conscience.

The primary religious meaning of childhood is to bring into existence the relationship of *father-son*. It is in these two words that the spiritual meaning of childhood becomes apparent, with its full religious value as a stage in life. The goal of childhood is to bring into existence (in the sense of realizing, giving shape to) a *father* and a *son*, a paternal and a filial relationship.

Seen from one aspect, the condition of childhood (the lack of an independent existence, the abandonment of oneself to another, the feeling of being in need) develops in man the *father*, in woman the *mother*. In this sense birth and childhood are gifts which the adult should accept with wonder, even if he does so in pain and faith as well. For they offer him a share in the absolute Fatherhood of God, the Creator of the world. Through the pain, danger, and agony of childbirth, parents are called to collaborate with Christ in re-generating the world, in bringing it to a new life, through His Pasch. Fatherhood is a providential grace through which man can enter into that fullness of love which is gift of himself to the point of sacrifice.

Fatherhood teaches man the true meaning of authority, which is neither demagogy, nor dominating another through superior strength, but rather service, mercy, and sacrifice. We would do well, in this context, to read again all the passages on authority in the Gospel. The quality of this fatherhood-authority will determine whether a true son of God and a genuine filial relationship come into existence.

From another point of view, childhood has as its goal to teach the *spirit of childhood* and to instill it into our flesh and blood as a permanent element. It is a privileged period, in which we experience dependence as the essential condition for a true affirmation of self, a time when we learn filial love, which is basically receptivity, faith, and gratitude.[5] In and through his own childhood, man learns to say "Abba, Father!" and thus to become, in Christ, the son of the heavenly Father.

The state of dependence, the filial love, and the proper love of self are not meant to disappear with the advent of maturity, for they should be enduring dimensions of life. Man must always, through one aspect of his being, remain the child that discovers, marvels, is in need, and gives thanks.

[5] "The real child according to Christ is the adult who, although surfeited with human glory, burdened with responsibilities, wounded perhaps by the experience of life, knows that he is never anything but a child to his Father. Adult in his own eyes and the eyes of the world, eternally a child in the eyes of God"—Liégé, *Adultes dans le Christ*, p. 12.

The religious meaning of childhood is to bring into existence a father and son according to God. The notions of father and son do not have their origin only in psychology. We truly know the father and son only in Jesus Christ.

Pre-Adolescence: Mistrust and First Hesitations of a Childhood Faith

Between childhood and adulthood, between son and father, there is the adolescent. Adolescence is nothing but a passage between these two stable worlds, an often difficult passage, "the narrow gate." We can distinguish three phases: pre-adolescence: roughly from 11 (12 for boys) to 14; pubertary adolescence: from 14–16; late adolescence: from 17 to 19–20.

In the overall context of adolescence the essential meaning of this first stage is to break with the closed world of childhood, especially with the world of the family, and to open the way to a more autonomous personal life receptive to the riches of the outside world.

On a psychological level preadolescence is characterized by vacillation between the security of childhood and the unpredictable impulses of adolescence. As the child leaves behind the rather limited world of the ten-to-twelve-year-old, his imagination is excited. Even though he looks back and is afraid, his instinctual drives push him irresistibly toward the unknown world of new sensations and ways of living. The butterfly throws off the cocoon in which he had been imprisoned and prepares to fly away.

Something similar happens on the religious level. Although he does not lose his faith, the adolescent tries to free himself from certain forms which his faith had taken during childhood. Seen positively, this means that his life of faith has the opportunity of becoming enriched with all the wealth of conscious reflection and greater personal autonomy of which he is now capable.

R. Guardini also

Everyone knows how severe the crisis of adolescent revolt is around the age of 14. It affects the adolescents' spiritual life, community life, and apostolic commitment.

From a psychological viewpoint, preadolescence appears primarily in a negative light, as a breaking away: the adolescent tries to escape, to break loose, to pit himself against the world of "Mother and Dad."

The same is true on the religious plane. This is primarily a period of doubt, of suspicion, of breaking away from the forms of childhood faith.[6] Little by little he cuts himself off from the environments which had nourished his faith until now (catechism class, priest, parents), and from certain childhood practices (prayers, going to Mass, etc.). Consequently he tends to become isolated, to be thrown back on himself, or into risky adventures.

If we analyze this general situation in greater detail, we shall discover the following elements:

First, there is a vague, oppressive drive of the instincts. It matters little whether the starting point for the upheaval of adolescence is a biological one. This much is certain:

[6] It is generally true that the appearance of the psychological phenomena of a given age has its religious repercussions only somewhat later. Thus among preadolescents their anxieties, attitudes of opposition, of breaking with their childhood world, will not at first be religious, but social or moral.

the boy of 11–12, who is active and extrovert, feels himself little by little invaded by instinctual drives which trouble him and threaten to cast him outside the familiar, safe world of his childhood.

Shaken by the impulse of new forms of sexuality, fascinated by the world of the "big guys," the adolescent thinks, says or does things that do not fit in with his family's views, or which are quite different from what he used to think, say or do until now. Hence a state of anxiety, insecurity, and guilt, which will corrode the "sacred" world of his Christian childhood.

Crises of scrupulosity are frequent in preadolescents; not even St. Thérèse of the Child Jesus escaped them. For instance: a child living in a Christian environment is filled with confusion and guilt because, challenged by his friends, he has for the first time dared to use a vulgar word, which on the lips of his friends seemed quite ordinary but severely shocked his family.

Worse than scruples: many young boys and girls live in a morose and dark anxiety, because they are invaded by ideas, imaginings and sensations relating to purity. Their feeling of sinning against chastity is considerably heightened through a sense of insecurity, loneliness, and isolation. In committing a sin they are unconsciously breaking with the world of childhood and parents.

As a result of a guilty, frightened conscience, and through fear of admitting their fault and being found out, many preadolescents give up certain religious practices which stand in their way—especially the sacrament of penance[7]

[7] This is even more true for girls than boys.

—and seek refuge in an atmosphere of anxious, morbid mysticism.

All these phenomena should be seen by educators in a positive light, despite their disturbing aspects. They often contain healthy reactions and always express a vitality seeking to define itself. In order that she could give to the world the revolutionary way of the "little road of childhood," St. Thérèse of the Child Jesus had to struggle to free herself from certain ascetic trends of her time.[8]

Second, there is a new susceptibility to influences outside the family. The drives which throw the preadolescent outside the nest of his family are stronger than his fears of the unknown and the disturbing effect of new sensations. He aspires secretly to discover the outside world, on his own, without the help of his parents. He wants to see and feel for himself, in order to "know" and "taste" this world.

Whereas the child was susceptible primarily to the realities of family life, there now awakens in the adolescent a keen sensitivity to the world outside his family: all sorts of infatuations—wanting to see certain movies, secret reading of forbidden books, etc.

At the same time there now appears a strong gregariousness that involves human respect and a keen sense of ridicule. Out of his desire to fit into the world he is about to enter, he will copy or conform to the reactions, ways, and attitudes of his environment. "Don't listen to the nuns," the older boys tell him, and this may temporarily keep him from going to Sunday Mass.

[8] Cf. Josef Goldbrunner, *Holiness Is Wholeness* (New York: Pantheon, 1955).

We cannot emphasize too strongly, especially in the case of implicit conversion or lapse, the decisive influence of the environment at this age. At no other time, perhaps, is he as open to outside pressures. The cause of this is obvious: because he wants to succeed with all the powers of his being, the adolescent will try to fit himself into the mold of social success. This mold is the whole complexus of relationships, love and hate, of prestige and currying favor that he finds in his environment. If he refuses to fit into the mold, he unconsciously feels that he refuses to grow up. After a first glimpse of the adventure of life, he will return to the closed world of "Mother and Dad."

In de-Christianized countries this is the most decisive crisis of faith for the adolescent. If the Church is linked in his mind, however slightly, with the world of his parents, he faces the following alternatives: either the world of priests (and parents), or the world of grown-ups, who no longer go to Church, and who "chase the girls." He must concretely choose between "staying little" or "growing up."[9] How can he be expected to choose a faith which, in his eyes, goes counter to the mainstream of life?

To this category belong all those adolescents who abandon a life of faith between the age of 13 and 15 because their parents have no Christian convictions, and they themselves have not found groups or institutions that can help them go toward a future which is both human and Christian.

[9] A typical situation in many Latin countries: you go to catechism class because your parents want it; you make your first communion "before losing your childhood innocence; THEN you become a man.

The situation is quite different for those who grow up in Christian countries or environments. Their life of faith will experience much less strongly the attack of worldly standards. They will quite naturally follow the example of those adults who have achieved a certain visible synthesis of faith and earthly commitments in their lives. In 1951 some young Canadians were asked to describe their dreams of the future. Several replied with a statement of this sort: "When I am grown up I'll own a car and modern machinery to work the land. I'll get into politics, and I'll raise money for my parish." Such testimonies are enlightening because they point up the link which exists in certain environments between different kinds of values: future, success, the Church.

The adolescent's whole being is straining toward the world of which he wants to become a part. It is easy to see that if the leaders of that world—sports idols, businessmen, movie stars—are Christian, the crisis of faith will be less grave, precisely because of this association (with all its ambiguities) between worldly success and the Christian life.

This association between Church and world no longer exists in France[10] as a whole today; the Church appears, rather, as a "poor orphan" compared to a world vibrating with life. To the adolescent this cleavage seems like a divorce.

[10] Although the situation here described refers specifically to France, this section has been retained because application can readily be made to the situation of the Church in the U.S. and other countries as well.—Trans.

On the one hand, he is hypersensitive to the glittering values of this world to which life is calling him, values that are different from those of the Church. On the other hand, the values of the Church seem to him out-dated and lifeless. Unless he discovers near him a living Christian witness, how is he to perceive the eternal youth of the Gospel? Life, for him, is to be found elsewhere.

As soon as the Church is in their minds situated outside real life, the standards of the world will quickly weaken the facile influence which the Church had over the altar boys.

A young man who was learning to fly told us: "Up there, the Church is far away. That's where life is. This is great, strong, exhilarating . . ."[11]

Conclusion

It was essential for us to stress this basic aspect of growth in the life of faith. In imitating more or less consciously the life of this world, making their own the values and morality of a pagan environment, young people imperceptibly and gradually find themselves far from a Christian way of life, "for they do not the truth." St. John did not grow weary of repeating: "My little children, keep yourselves from idols." Adolescents are particularly incapable of keeping themselves from idols when they live in the midst of idols—unless they have the balance of a Christian environment that is fully alive. Like so many adults who have remained adolescents, they identify the Church with certain structures.

[11] P. Babin, "La foi au terme de l'adolescence . . ." See, above, n. 2, chapter 2.

If young people are to climb successfully the slope of adolescence, they must have before their eyes the living evidence that they can serve God without turning their back on life. They need to see concrete instances of men and women who are fully human as well as fully Christian. And they must also find support in flexible structures that are adapted to our time (school, youth group, an atmosphere of friendship). When this is the case, when they have the benefit of a Christian environment that is open and missionary in spirit, when they are in touch with adults in whom they recognize a deep humanity as well as a living faith, then their spiritual life will develop and unfold quite naturally. They will readily take their place in the life of a fraternal community.[12]

Third, there is the crumbling of childhood supports. As he becomes aware of the outside world and as a more personal perceptiveness awakens in him, the adolescent realizes that there is a difference between the values of the world and of his family environment. Thus social conventions and financial worries do not mean the same thing at home as outside. Why should his parents be right?

Moreover, parents often refuse to discuss certain subjects with their children, such as love and sex. Frequently too— and this is more serious—the adolescent discovers that he has not been told the truth, or that his parents disagree

[12] We are thinking here particularly of certain parishes or youth movements where young people like to go because there is "room" for them to be at ease and relaxed, to express their need for a liturgical prayer that is truly communal, their liking for modern music, art, etc. They have a sense of balance in such communities, because they feel that they belong, in a synthesis of life and faith.

with each other. A girl of 15 said: "After my mother left us I saw how my father carried on with women; whom am I supposed to believe?" And if he discovers one fine day that a teacher whom he had respected or loved has sinned, he will experience in the depths of his being a terrible feeling of being betrayed. The loss of confidence in his teachers or parents wounds him in the very core of his faith; for these people whom he had idealized were in his eyes almost like God Himself.

It is easy to suspect the repercussions of such a situation and the feeling of insecurity that befalls the adolescent, in his spiritual life as well. He is too worried and timid to dare to ask questions, too jealously guarding his young personality, afraid of indiscreet teasing or merciless condemnation. He withdraws into himself and painfully broods over all sorts of questions without finding an answer.

Estrangement from his parents, loneliness, self-pity—this is the balance sheet. The supports of yesterday crumble little by little, while the guarantees of truth and good fall one by one from their pedestals.

A young girl of 15 writes: "First I laughed. I told myself that I was crazy to think of all this, and I tried to forget. Believe me, it wasn't a good idea, because now it's worse than ever. I am writing to you *because I can no longer stand being alone.*"

There is a positive side to all this: loneliness and interior confusion will become for many the occasion for deeply personal and intense reflection, the pledge of tomorrow's interiority.

Finally, in this climate of moral scruples, loss of confidence, new emotions and experiences, the first doubts and objections begin to raise their head. They are not directed primarily against dogma as such, but rather against the "why" of certain religious practices which the adolescent has traditionally observed since his childhood. "After all, why go to Mass, since So-and-So doesn't go? . . ." "Why go to confession, since I no longer know what is a sin and what isn't?" They will even go so far as to question certain doctrines which public opinion questions (such as hell), and which appear contrary to natural common sense.

Preadolescence thus appears chiefly as a neutral, negative phase; but also, in the light of tomorrow's conversion (which is our vantage point), as an absolutely necessary one. The caterpillar must leave his cocoon if he is ever to become a butterfly. The adolescent must break through the closed world of family relationships and leave behind the passivity and spontaneity of childhood. Only thus will the impetus of action, intiative and personal friendship awaken in him—an impetus which some day will become responsibility, conjugal love, fatherhood and motherhood.

Pubescent Adolescence: Excess of a Natural Piety and Instinctual Drives in the Light of Faith

Preadolescence is a predominantly negative stage, especially in two respects: The preadolescent tends to discard a passive attitude of naïve receptivity for an active one of freedom, separation, and destruction. At the same time he is inclined to reject, not the faith itself, but the forms of a faith he had unquestioningly accepted during childhood.

The second period of adolescence (14–16) is much more positive. Not that the ship has already come into port— No!; in the words of Giovanni Papini, the adolescent is a "Christopher Columbus without America"—but because he is setting out, searching, full of enthusiasm. The young person of 15 resembles an engine racing along without a destination. Where is he going?

First, and fundamentally, in the same direction as his natural drives. He is in pursuit of what is beyond him, impelled by the surging of instincts which are at one and the same time wounded and touched by grace, formed and deformed. Secondly, he strives after a measure of social success and conforms to the tastes of the day. This tendency will be still more apparent in the third stage of adolescence.

Emotional intensity, susceptibility to the tastes of the world, a natural and confused direction in his quest for God: such seem to us to be the chief traits which influence the adolescent's faith. He appears at this time strongly affected by his biological instincts. His reason and will are still imbued with natural—not to say animal—ways of thinking and feeling. More than ever he gives the impression of the "carnal man" of St. Paul, of man animated by an instinctual, autonomous biological drive.

We are particularly concerned here to see how this exuberance of the instincts affects the evolution of his life of faith. On the one hand, it delivers the superior powers of personality to the lower biological drives; on the other, it marks the life of faith with a strong natural religious sense, or sense of the sacred.

The realities of love or sex invade the adolescent's personality and carry him onto a slope of new sensations, enjoyment and egocentricity which tend to close him off from the knowledge and the will of God.

It is significant that at the outset of youth the world of friendship, of love and, in general, of all sexual realities is spontaneously placed outside of God and religion. Sexuality is surrounded by a whole climate of fear and anxiety, by an obsession with the need for enjoyment and by introspection, which throw the adolescent back on himself and turn him away from the true God.

Again, the adolescent instinctively rejects all constraint. He criticizes and opposes all forms of authority which controlled his childhood: the family, religious authority, the law and teaching of the Church. "I hate the word *duty!*"

In moments of strain he affirms himself as though he were his sole norm of existence. From this attitude it is only a short step to setting himself up against God. He talks endlessly about freedom, without realizing that what he calls freedom is in reality only a state of egocentricity and radical loneliness in which he adores himself as his own end and refuses all objective relationships.[13]

A young girl of 15 writes: "Right now, the times I like best are those in which I am not thinking of anything. Am I going crazy? I am becoming so independent that I hate everyone except myself. I'd be willing to cause a scandal if only people will leave me alone . . ." And another girl,

---

[13] The adolescent constantly and spontaneously confuses freedom with independence, freedom with license.

somewhat older: "I'm sick of constantly being in conflict
with myself and with God . . . Is there, then, no independence possible? Never? Nowhere? . . . Where is man's freedom? If I were free, I think I would have peace. I would
no longer be suffering, no longer be worrying . . . Why is
God such a tyrant, leaving us free to act only so that we will
not profit from it? Why has he given us freedom, since
we must give it back to him? This is the worst sort of
cruelty!"

This second text shows clearly the subjective imprisonment of the person, an imprisonment which leads logically
to the negation of God. Most of our adolescents will not go
so far, but will say instead: "Why was I baptized, why was
I brought up as a Catholic? Now I can't do anything about
it!" Or simply: "We are not free, since God knows what we
are going to do."

This overdose of instinctive subjectivity will mark the
life of faith chiefly in two ways. On the one hand, it will
lead to pagan ways of vanity, pride, and enjoyment. The
young person becomes the prisoner of forces which hold
and enclose him within himself, and which are accompanied
by an obsessive need to feel, e.g., "I stopped praying to see
if I would miss it" (a girl of 16). On the other hand, they
throw him into a confusion which discourages and disturbs
him. The excesses and lack of equilibrium due to the infatuations brought about by his instinctivity profoundly undermine the solid structure of his life of faith and leave
him at the mercy of great emotional insecurity. Often he
gives the impression that he is running around in search

of a savior. Take, for instance, the boy of 18 who writes: "I left school at 3 p.m. and met a friend. We had a drink. Then I took a cab to get home more quickly. I stretched out on my bed and listened to a record. Then I went to a night club. I tasted excitement and real life for an hour, but when I came out I was more disgusted than ever."

Let us not give way to an all too human fear. This painful experience of one's insufficiency, the failure of one's instincts and the disgust with life, all this can play an important role in the development of one's spiritual life. It is generally at this moment that many young people turn, from the depths of their misery, to the Church, to Christ the Saviour. Meeting a priest, a friend, or a group of friends can be decisive at this stage. Through such an experience many of them will come to a spiritual life which begins to be realistic, that is, which does not depend on the will of the flesh, but which is based on the acceptance of God through recognition of one's state as sinner.

A detailed study reveals that the religious behavior of adolescents is strongly marked by the sense of the sacred. Young people of 15 obey unconsciously laws of fervor or of religious indifference which are susceptible to the great forces of the sacred in its impersonal aspect. They pray before sunsets, meditate in a corner of a dark church, are enthusiastic about splendid ceremonies, experience a religious crisis at the death of a friend.

Instead of criticizing this susceptibility to the great natural symbols, we should try to discover their power of fascination, of sign and of call. At the same time we must

recognize their ambiguity as far as the faith is concerned.[14]

The cult of nature and mystic transports tend to take
precedence over the historical signs of Christianity. The
moments of enthusiasm and fervor, of rapture before the
grandiose forces of nature, are so strong that they imprison
the adolescent in the cult of religious feeling and cause
him to lose sight of the authentic religion of Jesus Christ
as it is lived in the Church. This has been referred to as the
"sentimental pantheism" of adolescents.

Instead of recognizing the priesthood, the Eucharist, and
the Incarnation as the concrete, historical and personal signs
of the Living God, they see only the universal signs of the
God of nature. They are carried away by the symbolic
presence of the Creator in the stillness of the snow, in the
intoxication of skiing, or in the magnetism of a crowd. It is
so much easier to feel the sacred presence of God driving
through the country than in church! Why, then, let yourself be shut in because of Sunday Mass?

The results of our study on the sense of God[15] show
clearly a lessening of explicit references to Revelation and to
religious instruction in school. These are replaced by the
subjective and naïve vision of the God of nature and of the
philosophers.

[14] "The faith of the child and of the adolescent will temporarily
borrow more than one trait from these 'faces' of God (of a childhood religion). It cannot be otherwise. Progress in faith consists
precisely in denouncing as inadequate or even false an adherence due
only or primarily to religious instinct, the sense of the sacred in
general, morality, or the desire for human security or for psychological peace"—Liégé, Adultes dans le Christ, p. 21.

[15] P. Babin et al., Dieu et l'adolescent (Lyons: Chalet, 1963).

Another characteristic of this period is that the religion of moral aspirations replaces a serious commitment of faith and charity. Once again, the inspirations of his heart drive the adolescent toward natural virtue and certain heroic forms of self-realization: endurance, generosity, idealism. He unconsciously confuses his own drives toward a rather vain self-perfection with obedience to God in the Church. The day comes when he becomes aware of flagrant discrepancies between "his own" religion and the "Catholic religion." This is the whole story of Simone de Beauvoir. She had been living in a world of idealism based on natural piety, and suddenly came up against the reality of a Church which she was quite unable to understand, so completely was she held prisoner of her subjectivity.

"From year to year," she writes, "my religion became more and more pure, and I despised the dullness of morality in favor of mysticism. I prayed; I meditated; I tried to feel the divine presence in my heart. In my spiritual books there was much talk of progress, of ascension, of souls who climbed steep paths and overcame obstacles. At times they crossed arid deserts, only to be comforted by a heavenly dew. It was all one great adventure. Actually, although I was growing intellectually from day to day, I never had the impression of coming closer to God. I longed for visions, for ecstasies. Meanwhile I lived without restraint, for my efforts took place on spiritual heights whose serenity could not be troubled. . . .

"One day my system received a rude shock. For the past seven years I had been going to confession twice a month to Fr. Martin; I used to tell him all about my mystic states.

He would react to my ethereal weaknesses with a sermon elevated in tone. One day, instead of conforming himself to this ritual, he began to talk to me in a familiar tone: 'I have heard that my little Simone has changed.' I flushed. I looked with horror at the impostor whom I had during all these years taken as the representative of God . . . I left the confessional with blazing cheeks, determined never again to set foot inside it. Henceforth it would have seemed to me as despicable to kneel down in front of Fr. Martin as in front of a 'scarecrow.'

"God came out of this adventure unharmed, but barely so . . ."

The key words are in the last sentence: God was not harmed. Indeed, Christ alone was wounded, along with Revelation and the Church. Only at a later date will she become aware of the inconsistency of the God of the philosophers and scientists; for the time being she needs him too badly.

At this time, too, the objections of natural reason to Revelation begin to appear. A young man writes to a girl: "I believe in God, in the God of creation, of the universe, of man. I believe . . . first of all because God wants us to be good; and then, because He has given us common sense, and because all that He tells us seems logical to me."

This boy describes very well the direction of his faith. It is not a question of accepting a Person who reveals Himself, but of a rational construction which relates to and justifies an element of childhood faith—the existence of God.

The same young man then gives voice to his doubts: "You want to know what I think will happen to me when

I die? A pile of dust, I suppose, like everyone else. The soul —immortal? If so, heaven and paradise? I don't think I really believe this. Are there such things as true happiness and eternal rest? It seems impossible to me, it's all very vague."

These doubts disclose the difficulty of ratifying or making secure with the help of reason alone dogmas that concern the Last Things. We have here in a nutshell the development of the adolescent's attitude toward Revelation. Faithful to his strong instinctual drives, he will naïvely ratify all that appears to him to agree with common sense and with the heart's natural impulses: God the creator, God who is the providence and end of man.

On the other hand, he will tend to reject or to question certain doctrines, insofar as they appear to him to be contrary to common sense or to the good impulses of his heart. We have here the conflict described by St. Paul between natural wisdom and the Wisdom of God, which is mysterious and hidden.

The adolescent's natural reason finds it particularly difficult to cope with the problem of predestination and freedom, the idea of mystery, the presence of Christ in the Eucharist. His "goodheartedness" is shocked by the problem of evil and of hell. A young girl of 15 writes: "To complete the picture, I'll tell you why I believe in predestination. It's not because I want to be different or draw attention to myself that I tell you this, but I express myself more easily in writing than in speaking. . . . Why does God give faith to some and not to others? Why is there so much misery in the world? People try to explain it to me, but

I don't understand. I assure you it's not because I don't want to. I'm sick of being the way I am."

And a girl of 18: "If God were God he would not have invented Satan. He would not have made the world so evil, and all men would be really equal. I can no longer make myself believe that God is really good. I don't want to be told that it's out of justice that He lets people be born who are blind, hunch-backed, mentally deficient—people who have done Him no harm; that more than two thirds of the population of the earth is hungry. I want to understand, and I want someone to explain to me why, if God is good, He permits evil and why, if the devil is evil, He does not forgive him and all his angels. . . ."

All these objections are still on the level of theory.[16] With some exceptions, this is not yet the time when the problem of evil presents itself in vital terms. Nonetheless, they undermine the building and prepare from afar either a rejection of the faith or, on the other hand, its purification and deepening through personal ratification.

Other objections, however, seem to be couched in more vital, concrete terms: they are directed against dogmas, and especially against the laws of the Church which seem to stand in the way of their desire for independence. "I dislike the Church for having taught me all these laws that keep me from doing what I want," writes a boy of 16.

[16] We can even say that they contain a strong element of play. This is proved by his failing to commit himself to the solution we suggest, or even to listening to the solution. Yet we must *pedagogically* go along with him, because he is playing a dangerous game which can lead him to entrench himself in pride or human solitude.

Such attitudes will be formulated intellectually only toward the end of adolescence. For the moment it is mostly a matter of moods, criticism, opposition, which will often lead to the decision to give up temporarily a certain religious practice. Thereby they prove to themselves that they are free, and that they are giving room to their expanding subjectivity.

We have stressed the negative side of the crisis of faith in adolescence, and the ambiguity of the instinctual drives. Let us not, however, forget all the natural wealth and enthusiasm which this age brings to its ardent quest for the Living God.

The impetuosity of the adolescent's religious tendencies can contribute to the maturing of his life of faith particularly in two ways:

Fervor: God loves His creation. God loves enthusiasm. God loves a full-bodied freedom. The adolescent's religious quest is only a beginning and a call. It is also a risk; but it is a privileged moment because of the intensity of the search and of the questions.

Character: the religion of childhood which was accepted unquestioningly does not suffice. Man must come to a personal religion, in which he knows himself by his own proper name in Christ's Body. The adolescent at this stage can bring to his life of faith all the wealth of his individual characteristics and temperament which begin to show themselves. God wants us to believe in Him with our own intelligence and with the blood that flows in our veins.

If the main tendencies of this age are channeled and

evangelized, they can then become open, with all their impetuousness, to the fullness of Christ who came "not to destroy but to fulfill."

Late Adolescence: Questioning the Life of Faith and First Stage of Stabilization

This age—between 16 and 20—marks a turning point of intellectual deepening and a first stage of stabilization. The confused movements of the drive of puberty are now succeeded by greater calm. Educators say that 17/18 is a golden age. If the adolescent is not impeded in his development by grave interior conflicts or led astray by the influence of adults, it is possible to discern in outline his future development—either commitment to Christianity or rejection of the faith.

The process of maturing takes place on a double level. Knowledge: his questions, doubts, and impressions will ripen and be purified by intellectual reflection. Will: thanks to the calming of his instinctual drives and to the process of intellectualization and socialization, his point of view will become more clearly defined and set in a given direction. These two levels obviously overlap in the complex interplay of intellect and will in the act of faith, so that it is difficult to distinguish them from each other. We are concerned here with the causes of maturing. On the one hand, the drives of puberty recede before a growing sense of realism and socialization. On the other, the intellect emerges from pre-adolescent turmoil, and begins to analyze and control the situation.

The process of maturing does not take place, however, without its share of drama. If it results in greater solidity, this goal is attained only at the price of battles, efforts and breaks with the past.

The process of evolution follows a triple rhythm, like waves that overlap: a state of doubt and deep insecurity; a state of reflection and intellectual deepening; a state of decision, commitment, emphasizing the direction chosen.

In analyzing each of these elements let us keep in mind that the division is only a theoretical one and that, in actual life, we do not find three distinct moments but rather three states—three waves which overlap and cover each other in turn.

First, there is a deep sense of insecurity attributable to the adolescent's greater awareness of his situation. Hitherto the adolescent's insecurity was above all affective, resulting from the incoherence and multiplicity of his sensations. The adolescent of 15 seemed to be at the mercy of his needs and moods.

"I am absolutely sick of it all," writes a girl of 15. "Maybe I would be less selfish if I could love someone . . . Yes, I feel the need to love someone, but if I talk about it at home they say: 'Oh, look at her, she's got a persecution complex! She thinks that no one loves her!' That's not it, I know very well that I am loved more than I deserve; but I need to feel that I am special, that I mean something to someone. I realize that I take myself too seriously, but I can't go on like this; I keep having dreams and don't know why, and I have fits of crying. Right now things are worse than ever. My sister is in love with a young man, they'll get married soon.

I have to admit that I am happy about it, but I am also jealous . . .

"You will be still more disgusted when I tell you that I feel like getting drunk! No kidding! I've become a materialist. I don't care right now. I want to get drunk in order to forget everything. I can't handle all these problems. I don't want to think about it anymore, and I don't want to cry in despair. . . ."

What a storm! She is so profoundly disturbed that she no longer knows where to begin.

And yet, this turmoil will gradually subside. At the age of 17 one is less at the mercy of one's feelings. The biological drives become less violent and a certain calm sets in. Nevertheless, the young person seems—in certain respects especially—more insecure, more distraught than ever. What is happening?

Through the tidal waves of adolescence the old forms of faith have become undermined. The intellect now emerges victorious over the sensations, but only to find that nothing solid has been built. Nothing takes the place of the structures that have crumbled. True, there is time to catch one's breath from the storm of feelings, but this respite only serves to pose more acutely the problems of commitment and building one's life. The chaos of puberty subsides, only to let a battered ruin emerge.

More acutely than before the question must now be answered: Who can help me make something of my life? In what direction should I build? For the adolescent this is a most urgent question, and it fills him with confusion. Faced with decisions that he must make, he realizes that his situation is anything but brilliant. At the same time his insecurity, which had until now been affective, becomes more and more intellectual and reflective.

Let us not be deceived: the crisis of faith at this stage is not—as it will be later—due to specifically intellectual problems, but rather to the awareness that his position is uncomfortable and very precarious. Whenever acute problems arise at this age it is nearly always under the shock of a love affair, under the weight of remorse, or even because of physical exhaustion. All these circumstances precipitate a keen realization that one's religious situation is precarious. This state of affairs cannot last. The adolescent is filled with the urgency of putting order into his life, with the need to see clearly, to breathe more easily.

"I am dating a girl of 16, and we often do stupid things together. Honestly, I don't understand what's going on, I don't even know if God exists. Tell me what's going on, please, help me."

Emotional shock, remorse, deep affective and intellectual insecurity—in these few words we have the summary of our analysis. Young people need someone who "helps them to see." They appeal not to a "maker of theories" who is able to prove the existence of God, but to an educator whom they respect, who understands "what is going on," and in whom they sense openmindedness.

As a result of failure, their intellectual insecurity quite frequently takes on symptoms of moral insecurity, for the young person experiences burning failures in his moral life.

As he grows up he realizes that the perfection of which he had dreamed cannot be attained at all, or only with great difficulty. In his work environment he comes up against social and moral failures, against the brutality of life. There is the danger that along with his dreams the last strongholds of his faith will also crumble. "What can I believe from now on? Not only is what I learned not true, but even what I had imagined seems to vanish."

For many young people such failures result in long periods during which they no longer lead a Christian life, and in practical despair which makes them conclude that God does not exist. For others, who are interiorly docile to grace and have the advantage of a truly Christian education, such failures will purify the adolescent voluntarism, opening them decisively to a religion of awareness of their brothers, charity, and acceptance of God.

In both cases, let us repeat, they have arrived at a turning point of the utmost importance. The necessity of a choice becomes clear: either a greater depth of faith, or lapse from the faith.

Adolescents at this time are given also to reflection and the consequent intellectual deepening. By the time he is 18 the adolescent's personality is already more developed. His scruples and fears about facing the outside world have become less acute, and the egocentricity of the drives of puberty gives way to a profound desire to find his place in society. His entrance into the world of work or of serious study marks an important turning point. The office boy brings home his first pay check; the young mechanic points with pride to the car he has repaired. They are men now, since they do the work of men. Success in a job or a college degree are passports into adult society. This social and intellectual challenge makes the young man or woman more susceptible than before to the ideas, principles, and views of the world.

We might thus say that their susceptibility to the world becomes intellectualized. Until now their openness to the world showed itself chiefly through a change in behavior. The adolescent's adoption of the ways of being and doing of the world led to a sort of "unconscious interior corrosion" of the values of his faith. Now, this corrosion becomes much more conscious and explicit. It is no longer only his attitudes toward life that are affected, but also the level of conscious knowledge.

A young man of 17 passed among his friends in school a statement which is typical of this intellectual maturing:

I am going to put the blame where it belongs. First, I want you to know that I am serious, I really mean it. I publicly, openly, purposely said what was in my heart at that moment. Some of you were shocked, others scandalized. I disappointed someone who had a different idea about me. Here I am naked; I have taken off the mask that was hiding my real face.

I came to school with a childhood faith. I thought about it and observed life. I read and re-read and studied the Gospel. I thought it all through and came to the conclusion that the Catholic religion is perhaps the ideal religion . . . on paper. I saw what was happening in practice: not one of you would say that you are non-Christian, but in fact you all live as though you are. When we pass Christians in the street, can we tell who they are? How many of them would suffer persecution for their faith? What makes your life Christian? A few cowardly gestures that have become meaningless, and that are repeated throughout the day . . .

Christ—if he ever existed—brought a superhuman religion, because he was a superman. And that's where he made his mistake, for the world is just the same as it was before he came.

I was still quite young when I began to ask these questions, but *they frightened me too much.* For a long time I did not want to face them; but today I want to be honest and sincere. I don't want to go on living in the soft lukewarmness of a small religion.

Only yesterday this young man had been disturbed by vague doubts and inarticulate questions. Today he formulates for himself, and for others, the stand he has taken. He has entered a new stage in his life.

These doubts, which he now dares to formulate, express the mind's inner processes. Throughout this intellectual re-evaluation there grows in the adolescent the desire to bring his practical attitude into harmony with his thoughts and feelings. He wants to be sincere. He is now strong enough to formulate his thoughts and to conform his conduct to them.

A boy of 17 writes: "Am I supposed to go to church, which is like a theater where everyone goes through the motions? I suppose some of the people there are sincere; but what disgusts me is that others play their role badly. I hate this hypocrisy. If I went to Mass and did not participate, I might as well not go. I am not trying to be original. It isn't that I want to pray in my own special way, but I do want to be sincere."

We find expressed here in extreme terms attitudes which

are not yet very firm. They are more like explosions, or cries
—so loud that they barely conceal the great timidity that
underlies them. And yet they give proof of greater reflection,
and hasten the coming of a dénouement.

During the first stage of adolescence we stressed the affective corrosion wrought by the prestige of the world. Here,
we must insist on the intellectual aspect of the "idols of
this world." The young person now listens to the mentality
of the world, to its classic objections against the faith, to its
maxims and slogans. The objections are always the same,
yet each period and milieu stresses a particular aspect.

In 1951 Fr. Guyen noted among Catholic high-school
students a susceptibility to the following objections:

How can God permit so much misery?	50.2%
One religion is as good as another	26.4%
Priests and Catholics are no better than other people	37 %
Religion concerns only my private life, it has nothing to do with my work, my studies	22.5%
I no longer go to Church because Father X said to me. . . .	27 %

In summarizing we find that the maxims and objections of
the world which are taken up by young people focus around
the following themes:

Rejecting the Church and her sacraments in favor of a
natural religion. A boy of 17 writes: "I don't need confession, I see no point in telling my sins to a man who is called
'priest,' who is chosen by others, indirectly by the pope, who

in turn is chosen by men." This is a typical situation: the young person considers Christianity as a natural religion, and he does not feel the need for the Church to practice this religion. On the other hand, he now understands that faith is not the result of reasoning.[17]

The scandals of priests and Christians provokes doubts. A young girl of 18 writes: "I see the way Christians around me live. I try to find real Christians, I look for love in them, for that assurance which their faith ought to give them; and I find nothing but egoism, pettiness, and a pretense of love."

Simone de Beauvoir analyzes her crisis as follows: "I was becoming caught in all sorts of contradictions. Neither my mother nor her friends had any doubts that the Pope was chosen by the Holy Spirit; and yet, my father maintained that he must not become involved in the affairs of the world, and my mother agreed with him. Leo XIII, in writing social encyclicals, had betrayed his mission. Pius X, who had not said a word about social affairs, was a saint. I had to digest this paradox: the man chosen by God to represent him on earth was not supposed to be concerned about the things of earth."

Whom is one to believe? The Church, or the common sense of one's naïve moral drives?

The problems of evil and freedom awaken metaphysical doubt about the very existence of God; the problem of free-

[17] When they plague us with questions about the Real Presence, etc., we must keep in mind how difficult it is for them to go beyond a purely natural and rational point of view. So difficult, indeed, that many prefer not to bring certain questions into the light of consciousness, because they seem so strange and incomprehensible.

dom is ordinarily linked to that of evil.[18] "Why did God create us, since He knew beforehand that men would deceive and betray Him? It seems to me that this is no longer goodness, but stupidity."

"I want to know the truth, but as I grow up everything gets more confused. Our consciousness is by nature weakened. Frankly, we have to admit that God has made a mess of creation. Until now I didn't dare to say it, I was afraid of blaspheming. But now I see that life is a scandal, that each man's destiny is full of suffering. How can I help doubting the infinite goodness of God?"

Thus the awareness of evil and of the failure of human freedom leads to the conclusion that God cannot exist. The doubts always follow the same road: objections are not posed in metaphysical terms (e.g., is there such a thing as freedom?), but in moral terms of happiness and human greatness. They see the uncertainty of happiness and the failure of human greatness, and they conclude that God— such as they imagined Him to be—cannot be called to account for this failure. Then comes the next question: Does God exist at all? A long education is needed to bring these young people to accept the true God of Revelation, who permits evil only out of respect for man's freedom and happiness.

Weakening of religious idealism and the violent need for happiness. "I love life in all its aspects. I want to live. . . .

[18] Except among those adolescents who have had more than a normal share of suffering, the problem of evil will make a real impact only around or past the age of 20. At that time it will have a ring of sincerity and personal suffering that is often deeply moving.

God, for me, will never be more important than my lover, my husband, my children, the beauty of life. Maybe He'll have a share in all this, but He will not be more important than they."

On the one hand there is a weakened religious aspiration; on the other, there is the growing desire for human happiness, for being part of the social order. God is very much in the way!

Skeptical attitudes and criticisms expressed by today's teachers. A college student comes to his chaplain at the end of a meeting: "The professor said in class that Christ was not the Messiah because the genealogy in the Gospels is wrong. He says it's the genealogy of Joseph—and Jesus is not the son of Joseph."

In places where the atmosphere and instruction are not Christian such objections will occur frequently. They are like so many pin pricks which, little by little, tear the cloth of faith. In the sphere of profane learning everything appears to be precise, solid, scientific, sure of progress and success. The realities of the world of faith appear to belong to another order, to a world that is intangible, perhaps even irrational. What are you to say to your history professor who, with his historian's prestige, demolishes in the space of a few minutes Christ's Messianic claim? What are you to say to your literature teacher, a dynamic, brilliant man, who discourses with evident pleasure on the morality of Rousseau and the philosophy of Sartre?

A chaplain at a technical school told us: "Young people have a thirst for the sciences which quickly makes them discover the gaps in their religious formation. They suffer from this more than we realize. It is often because they find themselves unable to answer certain problems that they start on the road of doubt, and eventually leave the Church." When in 1960 a group of chaplains organized a series of lectures on topics such as reason and faith, science and faith, they were attended by large numbers of students.

Whenever the teachers of this world, the leaders of an advancing science, oppose religion to progress or faith to science, Christianity suffers in the process. It is like saying: "If you want to be part of the future, progress, the real world, leave your faith behind. If you want to remain old fashioned, stay in the Church! The success of your life is at stake."

There is need, here, of precise, solid argument—otherwise they will not take us seriously. Yet we know very well that we are only stopping a breach in the wall which will be open again the very next day. We must lead our young people beyond a narrow apologetics into the true world of faith. In this way they will come to understand one day that the dialogue of faith is reasonable because it is interpersonal, but that it is situated far beyond reason and science.

Who is to tell them of the reality and seriousness of Christianity, if not men and women who combine competence in earthly affairs with a deep faith?

Awareness of the Church's ineffectiveness in the modern world. This objection is strongest among those who take the world seriously. For instance: a girl of 21 leaves the Church because she has discovered through her friends that the Church is ineffective in the world. "I work with X, who says he is an atheist. He helped me to see that Christianity is not effective, that the Church is out of date, and not worth bothering with. Just look at our world: Christians are outside the main stream of life. The Church is totally ineffective."

Objections such as these arise and take shape from the situations in which the young person finds himself. This last type of objection, which is particularly dangerous, is found chiefly among those who live in environments that are admittedly atheist.

We have insisted so far on those elements which are likely to shatter the adolescent's life of faith. We must also, however, emphasize the other side.

1) "Temptation" is not identical with "fall." True, temptation often seems to "lead to the ruin of many." At the same time, however, many young people come through it with greater strength, depth, and purity. In their case, temptation has fostered a more decisive, explicit evolution toward the Christian conversion of youth. This conversion would no doubt have been less painful, and would not have been marked by such a sharp break and commitment, if they had grown up in a more peaceful, sheltered environment.[19] We touch here the mystery of God's plan and of

---

[19] It is not a question of belittling Christian milieux and communities of faith, but rather of pointing out their failures and risks. An authentic environment of faith has nothing in common with a "hot-house" atmosphere. On the contrary, deep faith should make the environment more apostolic, more responsible and free in its Christian groups or structures. As it grows, faith should confront reality with increasing strength and depth.

human freedom. This much is certain, at any rate: the greater the appeal of the world's slogans to young people, the stronger also must be the appeal of the "slogans of the Church," or rather, of her deepest values.

2) At this turning point in their lives some young people are fortunate enough to benefit from a Christian formation and education commensurate to their needs. Take, for instance, this young man of 18, popular and good at sports, who said to his friends (a little naïvely but quite deliberately): "My faith is worth it. I don't see how the guys who've had our kind of education can fail to be Christians. We are free, happy. We know where we're going."

True, the growth in faith of these adolescents will also know its ups and downs. It will receive blows and go through critical periods, brought about especially by their instinctual drives; but their crisis will be less dangerous and dramatic than that of others who are exposed to all four winds.

In summarizing, we can say that this last stage of adolescence is characterized by greater understanding of the meaning of life, a deepening of the intellect and will. In general, the years to come will only confirm the attitudes formed at this time—unless the entrance into the world of adults and of work succeeds in upsetting a structure still too weak and dependent on a favorable climate.[20]

We must never forget that the entire subjective evolu-

[20] Entrance into the world of work or the university can lead to serious failure, particularly in cases where the education during childhood and adolescence was faulty, or where the support of a community is lacking.

tion of the adolescent's life of faith is directed toward the
D-Day of the conversion of youth.

And yet, choices ripen; attitudes become more pronounced. The commitments of faith show themselves—not
so much as the result of a slow, gradual illumination, but
rather by flashes of light and by sudden decision at the end
of a crisis. They can be recognized in a certain social relaxation of the adolescent, who finds himself more at ease in his
commitments, his friendships, or the youth group which he
has joined. Thus little by little, through events and encounters, through trials and the strong sensations of his instincts,
his whole life of faith has been deepened and purified.

As he advances toward young adulthood the following
maturational characteristics show themselves, indicating the
adult forms his faith will take: leaving behind childhood
supports, such as simplistic, subjective forms of his childhood faith; purification of certain artificial links between
the life of the Church and the morality of his environment,
secondary religious practices, nonessential forms of devo-
tion; recognition of the human and sinful dimension of the
Church on earth; consciousness of a personal vocation and
commitment of charity; feeling of intellectual security in
adhering to the objective faith of the Church. Not all these
characteristics, of course, will show themselves at one time.
Some will make their apparance only much later; but this is
the general direction of the process of maturing.

Whenever the evolution of the life of faith has been relatively easy and successful we can nearly always discern certain elements that played a decisive role: the adolescent

received an education in which he experienced both authority and freedom; he prays, and finds himself in contact with
a living community (an apostolic group, etc.); he has become involved in activities in which he gives of himself,
and which challenge his creative freedom and desire for
responsibility.

When, on the other hand, the life of faith has been abandoned, we notice the following factors: he has remained un-
touched (whether through his own doing or through circumstances) by the signs which proclaim the faith: the
Word of God, the life of the Church, Christian witness; he
encloses himself in hardness of heart, pride, self-sufficiency,
and a desire to be independent which enmesh him more
deeply in his subjectivity; he lets himself go morally, so that
he finds himslf outside the moral pale of the Church—in
adopting the ways of the world he has adopted the paganism
that impregnates them.

In general, the explicit abandonment of the faith will not
come as a decision at the end of a painful crisis of conscience, but as the effective recognition of the absence of
God in his life. "I live as though God did not exist. God
counts for nothing in my life. Therefore he does not exist."

Between these two paths of evolution—the one positive,
the other negative—there remains a third, an incomplete
path. Many young people never make the transition from
childish or adolescent attitudes to maturity, whether
through dissipation, evasion, cowardice, fear, or general lack
of maturity.

The analytical character of our study forced us to insist

on the dramatic aspect of the adolescent's maturing in faith. In the concrete situations of life this maturing often takes the form of an evolution rather than of tragic crisis. The interior realities, however, are the same: the adolescent is on the road toward the hour when he will commit himself to a choice long prepared for, which will henceforth determine his life—because God has at last become for him Someone who calls him by name.[21]

Spiritual Significance of Adolescence, and Lines of Evolution Toward Adulthood

We have said earlier that adolescence appears as a passage between the two stable worlds of childhood and adulthood. For the Christian, the word "passage" evokes resonances that go far beyond the world of psychology. Adolescence is the age of the Pasch; the age in which one is torn from easy securities and opened to the great battles of life; the age of discovering a "new earth"; the age of agony at leaving behind a familiar world; the age of personal decision. Do we not have here the basis for the whole mystique of youth groups and movements that challenge to an ideal, to commitment, to setting out on new roads?

Adolescence appears to us as the providential age of a spiritual passage or journey, which leads to a life of faith that is more *personal, reflective,* and *responsible.*

[21] As some psychologists have observed, the aspect of "evolution" is more important than that of "revolution," especially among Catholics.

This important evolution manifests itself primarily in three ways:

Attaining a personal reflective faith. The young person passes from a faith that he had accepted quite naïvely to a faith which is now received with all the weight of his reflective intellect and personal decision. This is the whole meaning of the crisis of faith which we have described.

Discovery of a personal vocation. There is also the passage from an implicit vocation, directed by parents, to a vocation explicitly known and personally willed. A personal clinging to God in faith normally crystallizes as we grow in an awareness of our vocation in and for the Kingdom of God. To believe in God, at the age of 20, is to begin to do your share of work in the vineyard of the Lord. It is generally recognized that the age of finding one's vocation is between 15 and 25. This implies, however, a deep interior maturing:

1) Becoming aware of oneself as a *unique person* (and not simply as the "I" of the child); coming to know one's potentialities and limitations.

2) Becoming aware of oneself as a *social being*, that is, of one's particular world of *relationships* with things and people; coming to know oneself in the various possibilities of having an effect on things (work); taking one's place in a world of personal relationships (likes and dislikes, friendship and love).

If the adolescent is to recognize himself as both an individual and a social being, he must first leave behind a world in which everything was taken care of and arranged by his parents. He has now discovered and taken possession of his own domain. He has recognized as God-given the basic orientation of his temperament, and the historical and sociological circumstances of his education, encounters and relationships. He has recognized, in faith, that he is committed. Is not the essence of vocation to set out into the future, conscious that God calls me by name?

Discovery of friendship. Whereas the family formed the privileged environment of the child, allowing him to develop almost exclusively filial and fraternal relationships, the adolescent rapidly opens himself to a new dimension: the love of friendship. He will make for himself a network of personal relationships rich in mutual equality, exchange and gifts, and desiring the good of the other.

Breaking once again the confines of his "I," he thus enters into a richer and vaster world of personal relationships. Having known filial love he now experiences the love of friendship, before coming to know, tomorrow, the love of fatherhood. He is providentially ready at this stage, thanks to his psychological evolution, to accept more consciously the mystery of the Covenant of Jesus Christ. He is now open—in a mutual exchange that is both tangible and spiritual—to the dimension of the Eucharist with all that it entails of grace, universality, tenderness, greater depth.

Adolescence constitutes a sensitive period for knowing Jesus Christ as Friend and the ultimate meaning of the universe. It is a passage through the depths, which will liberate

the young person from his selfishness and help him to live
as a friend of men in Christ, opening him more and more to
the full dimension of love in his earthly task.

The adolescent's entrance into adulthood is marked at
first by certain difficulties and trials which will rid him of
his remaining egocentric illusions and assure his stability as
an adult. After this he will enter—more or less rapidly, depending on people and events—the mystery of fatherhood
and creative responsibility.

The end of youth (or young adulthood: 20–25) termi-
nates a lengthy stage that is essentially characterized by
purifications from certain physical attachments and from
images that had been linked with faith. Now they must
gradually pass from enthusiasm to fidelity,[22] "to keep the
Word and bear fruit in patience" (Luke 3:15).

In leaving behind a highly subjective, enthusiastic period
of life in which he "dreamed" life, the young person now
finds himself ever more closely in touch with the whole
reality of existence. Little by little the world of objective insights will take on greater importance than the world of the
imagination.

One by one his illusions disappear, threatening to carry
away with them the drive and optimism of youth. How
many young families, after a first period of idealistic plans
and dreams, entrench themselves in individualism and
social egoism! How many members of Catholic Action,
weary of their initial enthusiasm and disillusioned, give way
to a practical materialism or to secret rebellion! We must
renounce the idea of an idyllic happiness of love, and dis-

[22] Liégé, *Initiation théologique*, III, p. 502.

cover the real nature of the other and the necessity of the Cross in personal relationships.[23] We must renounce the intoxication of success, the illusion of unlimited progress. We shall not be able to realize all our plans. We shall not elevate all of matter: for matter is dense and the sin of the world weighs heavily. We shall have to choose one road and renounce others, for it is impossible to plough every furrow.

Yesterday their energies were geared toward a success whose shape they themselves had determined; today, they begin to discover and enter into the intentions and ways of the Lord. The will to conquer is purified, and its impulse safeguarded by the dynamism of the Spirit. They have discovered in the service of others the highest affirmation of self, and their love becomes more and more an attentiveness to the other for the sake of the other. "Faith is more deeply impregnated with hope and becomes faithfulness" (Liége).

There is to be expected a passage from possession of self to abandonment of self under the forms of fatherhood and creative responsibility. The struggles of youth had as their chief aim the possession of self. Hardships and other battles were undertaken for the sake of human and social success.

The approach of adulthood had already made the adolescent more aware of the limitations of instinct and matter. With the awakening of the paternal instinct there grows in

---

[23] No matter how we present love, the adolescent's concepts will always have a certain dreamlike quality about them. For we find it difficult to accept the truth that the perfect realizations of our desires are only eschatological, that is, are not given us in this life. We can come to this realization only gradually, and through the experience of dying.

him the sense of total all-inclusive love, a love that is willing to let go of self for the good of others. Little by little there now stirs and unfolds in him the sense of life, including death, in order that life and resurrection may come to a multitude. At this moment the words of Jesus will take on all their meaning: "Father, I have finished the work You gave me to do. Now do You glorify me . . ." (John 17:4–5).

Such moments are no doubt high peaks which mark not only the coming to maturity, but genuine holiness. Nevertheless it remains true that the adult Christian has come out of the dreams and limitless realms of idealism. "He knows that he must leave behind his youth and think of death; he experiences the tragic at the heart of his existence" (Liégé). He knows, too, that it is not sufficient to be a cheerful companion and a fair-weather friend. He must assume responsibilities. He must be strong and persevering. He must plough his furrow and bring forth in pain.

The young adult resembles in some ways the child of 7–9. He has lost the subjective and slightly exaggerated enthusiasm of the young child and adolescent, and has not yet achieved the rather quiet stability of the adult who has taken stock of reality. He has measured life's possibilities and limitations. He knows other men, what to expect of them, and is aware of the price of love.

The young adult has strength of faith and audacity of hope; he is already learning the meaning of faithfulness and the taste of the Cross. He has embarked on the road on which he will discover that "there is no greater love than to give one's life for one's friends."

Chapter Four

Today's Youth

Much has been written about today's adolescents. The Christian does not always feel entirely at ease in this literature. The young people themselves are amused and annoyed at all that we write about them: these serious grownups, who study their cases with the help of all sorts of tests and surveys! It is not flattering to be treated as a case. And there is a way of moralizing on the "Case of X" which is thoroughly objectionable. Any judgment or psychological analysis that is devoid of respect for another person gives proof of a lack of morality in those who make it. The inner sphere of the human person is sacred, and man has a right to safeguard it. Moreover, it takes a great deal of love to understand, and to transform apparent weaknesses into potentialities.

Our study is delicate because of its very actuality. We shall begin with an objective analysis of psycho-sociological facts and motivations, and then proceed to brief confrontation of these facts with faith. We shall consistently refrain from anything resembling judgment, for we have no right to judge—not even in order to excuse.[1] If our analysis is on the whole positive, this is due not so much to human opinion as to a vision of faith. Reality is always positive when seen by Christ, in the light of His Resurrection.

Let us first consider the phenomenon of youth and its striking numerical growth. "We are the center and the heart. . . . The time can be told by our clock." These words of Péguy about youth are truer today than ever before.

In the first place, the number of young people has increased at a surprising rate. In his special message to Congress of February, 1963, President Kennedy said: "The annual birth rate since 1947 has been 30% higher than it was in the 1930's. As a result, the number of youth under 20 rose from 46,000,000 in 1945 to 70,000,000 in 1961. . . . At present birth rates, they will number 86,000,000 by 1970. . . . This year the number of persons under 16 years of age will be more than a million greater than last year, or an increase of 39%."[2]

Secondly, adolescence is growing in importance today because it extends over a longer period of time.

[1] There is a certain manner, in vogue today, that excuses everything—and which is due largely to the influence of psychology and psychoanalysis—that is basically contemptuous of human nature. Not to call "wrong" what is wrong is to despise another. It is noteworthy to observe adolescents' reactions in such cases: "I don't want people to feel sorry for me and to forgive me for everything," said one of them.

[2] Special message on the nation's youth, quoted in *The Christian Science Monitor*, February 5, 1963.—See also U.S. Bureau of the Census, Statistical Abstracts of the United States, 1962, 83rd Annual Ed. (U.S Government Printing Office, Washington 25, D.C.).

124

In primitive societies entrance into the adult world of the tribe was achieved abruptly and quickly, through various initiation rites at the end of puberty. It was sufficient to know how to hunt and fight with simple weapons. Today, this entrance into adulthood is considerably delayed for the majority of young people.

On the one hand they encounter difficulties in entering the occupational world because adults "hold on" longer than before. Medicine is extending the span of physical health, so that the age of retirement comes later than in by-gone days. On the other hand, entrance into the adult world requires longer study and training because of its growing complexity. Intellectual as well as economic factors make necessary more years of schooling.[3] Not only do you have to learn in order to maintain your place in the adult world, but you have also to find that place! Manual labor is replaced by machines, and the inexorable logic of this evolution will require a constantly growing number of highly skilled workmen, technicians, engineers, and specialists.

Paul Valéry already foresaw this phenomenon of youth when he wrote: "Adolescence is no longer a phase. It is an age in its own right." It constitutes a world in itself over

[3] ". . . in a paradox of supreme irony, we have lengthened the time of adolescence and yet shortened it as a period of effective psycho-social moratorium. We force our young to make a choice when society offers them little to choose from (or rather, too much . . .) and delay the attaining of the choice as long as possible while they are occupied with things that no one really thinks are very closely connected with their choice"—Andrew M. Greeley, *Strangers in the House* (New York: Sheed and Ward, 1961), p. 51.

which film producers, novelists, psychologists, and all sorts
of statisticians hover greedily.

We shall attempt here a survey of historical and sociological psychology, asking ourselves: What are the characteristics of today's adolescents? What is their attitude toward
the faith?

We can discern today a meeting of values that are common to the world of America and Russia, widely opposed
though the ideologies of these two may be: values of realism
and achievement. The Russian emphasis is on a strong
ideology that leads to action which unfolds according to
evolutionary laws, while the American trend, which is far
more human, stresses joy of life, material comfort, and
warmth of interpersonal relationships.

We have taken as our basis the results of a number of
studies which were verified by numerous personal contacts
with educators and adolescents themselves. The characteristics that emerged can be summed up under four headings:
1) their minds have been opened abruptly to new, unlimited perspectives; 2) they are suffering from an insecurity
which has painful repercussions on their emotional life; 3)
they display an astonishing vitality and sensitivity to human
realities; 4) they are becoming socialized.

Openness to Unlimited Perspectives

The most important characteristic of today's adolescents
seems to be the sudden opening of their whole being to a
new world of unlimited knowledge and possibility. Never

before in history, perhaps, has there been such a sudden phenomenon, with such vast repercussions.

The children at the beginning of this century generally knew only the familiar world of their parents or teachers, of their village or town; later, a job or profession. Their outlets for action were few and their means of communication limited.[4]

Fifty years later, in the same part of the country, young people are in touch with the whole world. Movies, radio, TV, newspapers, and magazines flood them daily with information and knowledge. Without having to move away from home they discover technological achievements that disclose dizzy and limitless heights of the human spirit.

Why should a young man remain shut in by his environment, when he sees on TV the success of his peers in sports or the arts in New York or Japan? Why should the young engineer, who has already measured the power of his machine, not ask for still more powerful machines and for automation? Why should the young farm boy remain tied to his land when he sees on TV the endless lines of cars that drive out of New York or Paris on a weekend?

It is difficult for us to imagine the psychological turmoil produced by this sudden opening up of a world taking shape before his very eyes, and by the many new possibilities for action available to him. A young engineer interviewed in France said: "Thirty years from now we won't recognize our planet. There will be new countries; others will have disappeared. To remain behind, to go to sleep, will mean being

[4] *Our Town* by Thornton Wilder is a classic American example of such a "stable" way of life.

relentlessly crushed. Maybe this is why you take us so seriously." And another: "Meanwhile the face of the world is changing. You think that everything will turn out all right, but we think that your optimism has no basis at all in a world that is being turned upside down—in a world from which we don't intend to be excluded . . . We are determined to break down the walls if necessary, to throw out all the old ideas and routine."

Man has also discovered his own dimensions in time and space. Paleontology teaches him his origins in the earth; ethnology and the history of religion or art bring to light his remote origins. Thus he is able to construct for himself a provisional synthesis of the human species and of its slow development in history. All this wealth is put at the disposal of young people in the classroom, through magazines, radio or TV.

There is more yet. Yesterday man was made by history; today he in turn makes history. He is no longer at the mercy of the waves but has seized the helm. He knows that the march of history depends first of all on him, and he has measured his resources. Projecting into the future his own dynamic vision he sets about controlling the earth. Will he be able to make it into a paradise?

Although Marxism may unduly monopolize and falsify these perspectives, they can be discerned as a sort of common denominator in the spirit of modern man. They are more strongly embedded in the souls of adolescents than of adults, for it is the former who will build the world of tomorrow. "Don't you understand that we are part of a great movement, as big as the planet? Don't you see the thou-

sands of young people coming into all areas of modern life
—astronautics, nuclear physics, electronics, cybernetics, to
name only a few? And not only here in France, but in the
United States, in Soviet Russia, in Communist China.
Young people no longer resemble their fathers. You hardly
know what they are like, and they don't believe in your set
of values."

We may consider the consequences of this turmoil by
viewing the extremes of the new trends: rebellion and
emancipation. The vehement rebellion of juvenile gang
members that regularly fills the newspapers and alarms the
public is in our opinion due first of all to this phenomenon
of the sudden opening up of knowledge.

A "leather jacket" in one of the main streets of Lyons explained to a friend: "You ask why I am the way I am? I'll
tell you. It's easy enough to figure out. Once I saw a college
boy come out of a night club. He took a pack of American
cigarettes out of his pocket, lit one, took a couple of drags,
and threw it away. Well, I can tell you that I felt like beat-
ing him up."

What do we have here? A young man who lives in poverty
and want. Contrast with this the arrogant ease displayed by
an affluent society. Moreover, TV programs and movies
have taught him violence and aroused in him the desire to
be "tough." How can he resist?

We find among lower-class youth today an attitude of rebellion that frequently leads to evasion, nervous depression,
and complete disillusionment. The gap is too wide between
their dreams and aspirations and the inhuman conditions in

which they find themselves. There is much talk of leisure, comfortable homes, success and money—and yet they continue to lead a miserable existence in tenements.

Statistics show that many of them have a growing interest in study and evening classes; yet they become aware at the same time that they have no future as unskilled laborers, that their lives will be spent on the fringes of society. This generation is more painfully aware than previous generations of the discrepancy between what they could do and what they actually are doing, between what they could be and what they actually are. In the address already quoted President Kennedy said: "Youth unemployment is an increasingly serious one. Unemployment among young workers today is 2½ times the national average. . . . During the 1960's. 7,500,000 students will drop out of school without a high-school education . . . entering the labor market unprepared for anything except the diminishing number of unskilled labor openings. In total, some 26,000,000 young persons will enter the job market for the first time during this period, 40% more than in the previous decade."[5]

In contrast to the more unfortunate ones who are in violent revolt, there are the suburban teenagers. They have money and opportunity, which make them radically different from the others. They have grown up in comfortable homes, but without knowing the healthy, disinterested atmosphere of true love. Their fathers are busy getting ahead in their professions, their mothers are always entertaining to

[5] This is also the main theme of Paul Goodman's *Growing Up Absurd* (New York: Random House, 1960).

keep up. Parental authority is not totally absent but permissive, and that is why they are often driven to vehement behavior.

Yet they too experience the trauma of the sudden unfolding of the world's limitless possibilities. Formed by an education which does not face up to modern currents, sure of themselves and in control, they cannot but yield to the frenzy for pleasure that takes hold of them. They have no scale of values to which they can refer.[6] They want everything indiscriminately: records, money, love, convertibles. And since they are among the lucky ones, they can own everything, try out everything. They too will become rebels and throw off the yoke of moral principles or social mores.

A new mentality has been created by the new development of knowledge; and it has stirred up man's desires. The great theme of the modern world is not the problem of evil (as it was during the Middle Ages), nor the problem of grace (as it was during the seventeenth century), but happiness, success. The Reader's Digest and magazines of all kinds flood us with the secrets of success and eternal youth.

Parallel to this theme is that of the conquest of nature and the domination of the world through science and technology. Here again, we cannot overestimate the appeal which this perspective of man's godlike power and his access to vast new worlds holds for adolescents. Our grandfathers would have laughed if we had told them that some day a jet

[6] Elvis Presley, Françoise Sagan, Brigitte Bardot all seem to have enjoyed an education as children that was relatively free from problems. Child prodigies or spoiled children, they were to say in later life that it was at home they felt happiest.

plane would break the sound barrier in flight from New York to Paris.[7] Could a previous generation have imagined the day when we can go to the moon? Such perspectives, which today have become reality, throw them into skeptical amazement.

These developments do not worry young people, however, but rather confirm their faith in man. Moreover, they believe that the present organization of the world is not in line with the evolution of science and technology. In their technological realism they dream of a leveling of society which would assure to all men and peoples an equitable share in human happiness and the world's resources.

If nature has ceased to be an object of fear for them, it has also ceased to be an object of contemplation. Nature is simply a fact which man tackles in order to control, make it safe, bend it to his service. The world is a vast enterprise which man can and will construct.

It is because they know this and think themselves able to carry out realistic reforms that many young people abandon idealistic social causes. They espouse instead rightist or individualistic positions of evasion, or fail to commit themselves politically.[8]

Such a view of the world will obviously affect greatly the lives of young people. Let us bring together the elements of

[7] Maurois writes: "Soon the child will say, 'Mother, I'm going to the States.' His mother will reply, 'Take your lunch along!' "

[8] This trend appears clearly even in literature. The committed art of a Sartre or a Camus is no longer in vogue; rather, there is a trend toward a more "uncommitted" estheticism, apolitical (Sarraute, Genet, Samuel Beckett, Ionesco, etc.), which has something in common with the literary tradition between the two World Wars.

our inventory: 1) unlimited aspirations for knowledge and happiness; 2) a sharp break with the older generation; 3) an objective sense of reality acquired through science, a sense of man's power over nature and the earth; 4) a tragic disproportion between the possibilities they envision and the concrete realizations that are possible.

What does all this mean for faith? The phrase "Dionysian temptation" has been used with reference to modern man. Are we not witnessing today a phenomenon which resembles the Renaissance, though it is more vast? The Church is traversing a period of history fraught with possibilities and dangers. Possibilities: the time has come when the Church must make her own a new dimension of reality. Faith must be enlarged by the new horizons of human achievement. Dangers: each new discovery threatens the integrity and intimacy of the mystery entrusted to the Church by Christ. The danger above all others is the temptation to pride and self-sufficiency. Man today must radically choose between the solution of Nietzsche and Sartre to make himself into God, or the Christian solution of offering his creative drive and love for life to the Lord of Life, who is their source and ceases not to bestow them on man.[9]

One thing is certain: the opening up of so many new vistas, with the doubts and questionings that come in their wake, tears this generation from the lukewarmness of ready-made solutions. In entering upon a new stage of maturation, mankind is forced to a choice that is more lucid and coura-

[9] These perspectives are taken up again and developed below, in the context of positive orientations (pp. 185 ff.).

geous—unless, indeed, men harden themselves in a cowardly refusal to face reality.[10]

Insecurity and a New Way of Living

"Have no doubt, it is fear in her eyes. Have no doubt, it
is fear now in his eyes also. It is fear, here in this house,"
says Alan Paton in *Cry, the Beloved Country*.

These words, which try to express the state of mind of
both Europeans and Africans in South Africa, can be ap-
plied to today's adolescents. A deep insecurity about themselves and the future haunts the young generation—whether
we think of a James Dean, wounded and vulnerable, of the
"hood" who is abnormally gaunt beneath his leather jacket,
of the suburban teenager keeping himself busy at anything
and everything so that he won't have to think, or even of the
leftist idealist or rightist reactionary, who compensate for
their failures by being aggressive.

As Karen Horney has diagnosed quite correctly,[11] anxiety
is the disease of our time. The feverish desire for activity,
craze for speed, fascination with whatever is new, desire to
see the world, mad rush to escape on vacation, and finally a
brutal, awkward self-assertion—all these are often nothing
but masks behind which man tries in vain to hide his profound insecurity. He is afraid to look at himself, afraid to
live with himself.

[10] Existentialism and Marxism have at least this in common with
Christianity (even though their metaphysical outlook separates them
profoundly): they would bring man to confront in earnestness and
with lucidity the great problems of life. Even so, will not serious
commitments remain limited to a tiny minority?

[11] Karen Horney, op. cit.

Gertrude von le Fort, for her part, has diagnosed with great insight the phenomenon of "masculinity" which characterizes our time. The hyperactivity of building and domination are in her opinion the consequences of a general lack of love from which today's adults were the first to suffer. Those who did not experience affection in their childhood will always feel very much alone in life.[12] Because they have never known love, they will know only how to dominate or run away. No matter how much a person may seek to avenge himself of this frustration by alienating himself entirly in his "will to power," he will remain wounded in the core of his being.

In his Christmas Message of 1957 Pope Pius XII evoked a similar picture of modern man when he spoke of the tragic insecurity of our world as the great suffering of this time.

We might think at first sight that the insecurity of today's youth is due to the recent discoveries of science or to the H-bomb. Studies that have been made show, however, that this is not the case. Psychiatrists have clearly demonstrated that the state of "stress" and violence is due either to the many severe shocks which assault men today without respite, or to their inability to react to these shocks because there is no one who can help or reassure them.[13]

[12] Unless later, e.g., in marriage, or in a profound Christian purification, they are "re-born" through being loved by someone.

[13] Cf. the studies of the Canadian doctor Selby on "stress" and the phenomena of adaptation of the subject. See also the studies of Spitz and Liddel. The latter tell of a typical experiment: Take 2 twin goats, put them in two rooms that are exactly alike; the one remains alone, while the other is with its mother. The one who is alone is brought regularly to its mother to suck, then taken back to the room and left alone. The two kids are then put through the same

The insecurity of today's youth has these two related causes at its source: too many shocks and the absence of dependable authority.

First there are the brutal shocks and the profound upheaval which the chaos of noise, sensations, new ideas and facts produces in young people. We can hardly imagine what it means for a young girl or boy from a small country town to be suddenly transplanted to one of our huge modern cities. A college student said of her professor: "I am confused and frightened because he has new ideas all the time." Another: "I feel like a little kitten lost on Fifth Avenue."

If it is true that each generation through heredity passes on to the next all that it has learned, then the child born today finds himself at a great disadvantage. For he must suddenly face all sorts of concrete situations which his parents have not known. From the deafening noise of the modern city to the complex machines which penetrate to the remotest corner of the countryside, he must sort out hundreds of sensations, classify new images, answer endless questions, and learn all kinds of new reflexes.

Besides the shocks that assault the adolescent while he is trying to become a stable person, there are others that undermine his trust in his fellow men. Nothing wrecks our inner resources as effectively as witnessing the destruction of harmony and solidity in our human relations.

---

experiment, repeated at regular intervals: the light in the room is put out for 10 seconds, and during this time the two front legs of both are given a slight electric shock. After a short time the kid that had been alone is dead. The autopsy disclosed a severe dehydration (result of emotional shock). The kid that had remained with its mother, on the other hand, survived without any harm.

American young people do not bear the scars of war, social revolutions, concentration camps and deportation, as does the new generation in Europe and other parts of the world today. Yet their insecurity is no less deep, for the double standard of morality that frequently prevails among their parents and other adults, the lask of respect for purity, the cheating and stealing in school—all this serves to undermine their trust in their fellow human beings.[14]

If young people have been surrounded by warmth, security, and protection in childhood, they will learn new ways of behavior more easily and pass through a lax moral atmosphere with less anguish. The young tree that grows up in the shadow of the old oak is not afraid of cold and the wind. Many children today, however, lack this protection. They are born into a world of adults who are themselves too confused, too lacking in a center of gravity, and are so engaged in their own flight from reality that they are not able to give their children that resting place and safe harbor, and especially that loving attentiveness, which they need.

The drama consists in this: in a world which is evolving at a dizzy rate the child must make his own way, find solidity and roots all on his own. His parents are far from him, overworked, worn out by worries and activities. As Spitz has shown,[15] the best medical techniques will never replace

[14] In J. D. Salinger's *Catcher in the Rye* Holden Caulfield's search for sincerity typifies this rebellion against adult "phoniness."

[15] Cf. the works of R. A. Spitz on the traumatic results of separation from the mother. See especially "The influence of the mother-child relationship and its disturbances," in K. Soddy, *Mental Health and Infant Development*, Vol. I.

a mother's loving care for her child in ensuring his emotional and physical equilibrium.

Let us single out here one point that has particularly serious consequences: the abdication of authority. While it is true that the failure of authority in education can always be attributed to egoism, carelessness, or inadequate training, there is the additional factor today that parents have been shaken in their own security as educators. The questioning of so many values and pedagogical methods has left them disconcerted and has frequently led to their abdication of authority. Parents suddenly recognize themselves in radio programs and feature articles that lay bare to a wide public the secrets of complexes and frustrations. They fail to realize that the portrayal is often extreme and does not necessarily fit their own situation. They develop guilt feelings and abandon the ship in despair—unless, of course, they react in the opposite way and become set in despotism and constant nagging that are no less harmful.

How can parents or educators guide the awakening aspirations in their children, when they themselves are in the grip of doubts and hesitations?

Thrown into life without a guide, disconcerted by economic, social, political upheavals, undermined by a multitude of physical and psychological shocks, today's young people shut themselves up in a false realism directed toward people, institutions, and ideas. It is based on what they themselves are and on what they touch.

On the one hand, they instinctively mistrust empty phrases and abstract ideals; they have little patience with philosophical arguments and hero worship. On the other, they cling tightly to objective facts, to the effectiveness of action, to the firm ground of their own experience; for this is the sort of realism that pays off!

Young people today no longer feel the existential anguish typical of the postwar era. The tragedies of the war are already too far behind them to arouse agonized questioning. They have abandoned the attitudes of dangerous aggressiveness, defiance, and revolt against traditional structures, because they have confidence in their own view of reality and are more concrete, more direct in their proccupations. Their insecurity becomes instead a hard, practical conformism and cynical acceptance of reality. They take life as they find it, without romantic illusions, very much aware of the relativity of things.[16]

The cult of ideas, doctrines, and heroes is succeeded by the taste for the concrete, for understanding people, as well as by the great need for a familiar, safe world in which there is room for dreams and evasion of reality. In extreme cases they flaunt their egocentricity and exclusive reliance on the here and now.

"You want to know what interests me most? Myself. What interests me least? Other people."

"Our generation won't be fooled by fancy words." — "What matters is getting ahead." — "I don't know where I'm going, but I *am* going." — "I can't stand people who put on an act!" — "I don't believe in heroes. If they exist at

[16] The terms "de-romantization" and "de-sacralization" have been used. The novels of Sagan are typical in this respect, because of their taste for conciseness, truthfulness, avoiding all that is sentimental.

all you're more likely to find them among the firemen than the soldiers!"

Father Andrew Greeley writes: "In the early 1960's we Americans do not want heroes. . . . The reaction to Doctor Thomas Dooley is a perfect example of our contemporary indifference to the hero . . . When Dooley died, a lot of people wept, but there weren't many who wanted to take his place. . . . In 1927 the public identified itself with Lindbergh. The young could see themselves performing similar feats when they got older. The old would have liked to see their children accomplish something akin to what 'The Lone Eagle' had done. But precious few Americans want to go to Laos to heal the sick. . . . As a nation, we admired Lindbergh and wanted to imitate him; today we are still fascinated by Tom Dooley and cheerfully contribute money to his cause. And so the hero vanishes and is soon forgotten."[17]

Here are a few examples of the answers given by adolescents when they were asked what they wanted to get out of life:

X at 15: "I'll have a big house with beautiful furniture. I'll retire at 50 and live in the country."

X at 15: "I want a comfortable old age."

X at 16: "Money, no worries, a peaceful existence."

X at 17: "I want an easy life, movies, money and women."

X at 17: "I don't care what kind of work I do if only I make money."

Once the explosions of adolescence are past, the terms "success" and "self-development" quickly become key

[17] *Op. cit.*, p. 20.

words, replacing the great idealistic dreams of the postwar world. This is shown in the following statement of a Catholic college student: "I've made up my mind, after a lot of thinking, to *succeed* no matter what, and to make a good life for myself. I don't mind saying that I intend to use all my talents and drive to become a *professional success*. I have decided once and for all to *succeed*."

"It's all very well to be attractive, to love and be loved, but it isn't enough," someone wrote about the young novelist A. M. de Vilaine. And a young girl whose parents were divorced said: "I have suffered too much because of my parents. I am going to love my children and give them the right kind of upbringing." These seemingly commonplace statements could summarize the way young people live today. Too realistic and disillusioned to tackle metaphysical problems and great ideals, they conceal their uncertainty and lack of roots in a safe, concrete pursuit of human relations, and tangible success at home, in their job or profession.

The search for security and stability, a fair measure of happiness in a mélange of seriousness, realism, and evasion —this is the new equilibrium or, as it has been aptly called, the new "art of living" they want.

On first sight such a picture might appear rather gloomy for the future of the adolescent's life of faith. Is this really so? We believe, on the contrary, that if young people today can find what they are half-consciously awaiting they will become part of the renewal sweeping through the Church. The return in our time by many young Catholics to evangelical values indicates the course we should follow:

We have said that adolescents are tired of ideas and big
phrases. But, we may ask, is Christianity an idea or *event*?
The trend toward realism today can bring about a providential turning toward the true religion of Jesus Christ.
Educators who have worked to form adolescents through
the apostolate or an enlightened catechesis are aware of the
seriousness of their commitment to Christ and of their
aptitude for finding God in the event.

Young people suffer from a deep insecurity and lack of
love. Is not Christianity essentially the Revelation of Love?
Is not the Church the source and place of the true community? Is not Jesus Christ the "gathering of brethren"?

True Christian educators, who proclaim Jesus Christ in
word and through a life lived in charity, know how completely young people are "re-born" 'in hope and made new
when they realize that they are loved personally and deeply
by Jesus Christ today.

Thirst for Life, and Sensitivity to Human Values

Since the 1940s we have witnessed an unchaining of the
instincts on all levels, to the detriment of the intellect and
reason. How these facts are to be interpreted is the crucial
question.

Let us start with the most ordinary level: young people's
love of cars. They crave speed, to which they are willing to
sacrifice comfort. Here are the results of a typical interview:

"If you had money, what kind of car would you buy?"

"A Lark."

"Why?"

"Because it's fairly inexpensive to run and handy for city driving."

Another replies: "A Thunderbird."

"Why?"

"Because of its design. . . . And I love speed."

"Would you be willing to give up comfort for speed?"

"You bet!" (a quite general answer).

Another: "A Jaguar."

"Why?"

"Because of its streamlining. I love speed, and I go crazy when I race the motor."

Intoxication with speed, need for power, streamlined design! James Dean's words are well-known: "I go faster than the wind, I go faster than the blood in my veins. I go faster than the waters of the Mississippi."

This is true not only of their love of cars and whole way of life, but also of higher forms of expression such as painting, music, etc. A study of Picasso's paintings reveals the unchaining of instinctual forces like aggressiveness. When Jean Cocteau decorated the Chapel of Saint-Pierre he hoped to provoke a reaction against what he called the "taste for the monstrous and the fascination with the nightmare." His manifesto, however, which claims to re-instate the values of the intellect, did not create a great stir. Perhaps it is still too early?[18]

In the realm of music their preference for brutal, abrupt rhythms is strikingly evident. How else can we explain the

[18] *Album photographique: La chapelle Saint-Pierre.* Introduction by Jean Cocteau.

success of Rock 'n Roll among teenagers, or the popularity of Mahalia Jackson and Odetta among college students?

In a 1958 interview Jack Kerouac told a reporter that jazz is the music of the Beat Generation because of its violent rhythm, which "takes you out of yourself." Here is a selection from his book *On the Road*: "Uproars of music and the tenorman *had it*, and everybody knew he had it. Dean was clutching his head in the crowd, and it was a mad crowd. They were all urging that tenorman to hold it and keep it with cries and wild eyes, and he was raising himself from a crouch and going down again with his horn, looping it up in a clear cry above the furor. A six-foot skinny Negro woman was rolling her bones at the man's hornbell, and he just jabbed it at her, 'Ee! ee! ee!'

"Everybody was rocking and roaring. Galatea and Marie with beer in their hands were standing on their chairs, shaking and jumping. Groups of colored guys stumbled in from the street, falling over one another to get there. 'Stay with it, man!' roared a man with a foghorn voice. . . Boom, kick, that drummer was kicking his drums down the cellar and rolling the beat upstairs with his murderous ticks, rattlety-boom!"[19]

All this is reminiscent of the "vita est in motu—life is in motion" of scholastic philosophy! No doubt we have here a vitality that is largely biological and radically deformed. Yet all this agitation, this frenzied living, are symptomatic of an acute crisis of suffocation as well as of an immense thirst for life.

[19] *On the Road* (New York: Viking, 1957).

Through the unbridling of their instincts young people are tragically searching for an absolute, a way to get out of themselves. On the other hand, such exuberance may also express their need to define themselves, to experiment with their own sensations in an excessive enjoyment.

Through all this the adolescent tries to compensate for the deep wounds in his innermost being. He is suffocating in a world without soul, overwhelmed by a life that is comfortable but devoid of spiritual joy. He remains lonely, insecure, and rebellious in the anonymity of a rational, technological society. A twenty-year-old student says: "I am sick of my parents. Life is empty. I feel like getting out of this world, and I dance Rock 'n Roll."

Weary of an inhuman, impersonal existence they seek a first door of escape in a tumult of instinct which has as its aim oblivion and ecstasy. They find a second door of escape in camping and sports, in going "back to nature." In our time of comfortable homes and innerspring mattresses, what a relief to go skiing, to drive with the top down, or to lie on the beach and cultivate a tan!

In his novel, The Roots of Heaven,[20] the odyssey of a young man who goes to Africa to defend the herds of wild elephants threatened with extinction, Romain Gary writes: "I believe in individual freedom, in tolerance, in the rights of man. . . . I will defend them (these wild animals) to the end against the outbursts of men drunk with racism, nationalism, lust for power. No theory, no argument, no

[20] Romain Gary, The Roots of Heaven (New York: Simon and Schuster, 1958).

ideological camouflage will make me forget their superb simplicity."

The life of free animals! Man needs to feel the throbbing of this enormous, awkward freedom, says Morel, the hero of the book. Dogs are no longer enough for him. The adventure of life must unfold against the whole of living nature.

While such expressions or desires reveal abiding needs of human nature, they have become more noticeable in recent years. We must pay a price for living in a society that is soulless, without security, or love. In such a world the unconscious mounts to the surface and the instincts take their revenge.

This too-animal instinctivity is not without moral consequences. And while it will generally become somewhat subdued toward the end of adolescence, it will leave behind deep scars. It will live on in the taste for sensation, the desire to experience in order to understand and believe, and above all in the cult of independence and the exuberance of life.

Y. Thireau stresses quite rightly the unbridling of the need to feel and see. He analyzes its causes and disastrous effects on the intellect and nervous system:

"Just as the eye does not perceive an object that passes too rapidly in its line of vision, so too man can neither distinguish nor analyze a given problem if too many problems follow each other and demand his attention. There are too many things to be seen and done, and modern man cannot think as fast as objects present themselves to him. Among *adolescents, consequently, the thirst to know is replaced by the thirst to see everything.* They adopt a rhythm which wears them down all the more rapidly because many of them are already physically unfit. Every nervous tension should be followed immediately by a period of relaxation, so that the muscles can relax; but there is no time for this today. I do not say that young people are really physically active all day long, far from it. But even when they are passive they must put up with the blare of radio and TV, the noise of the street, the aggressivness of advertisers. Through no fault of their own they follow a modern criterion: 'Let's sacrifice everything to speed.' . . . They have no choice. Our modern tempo of life forces on them so many movies per week, so many magazines, songs and TV programs, etc."

Can we imagine the consequences which such a situation involves for the religious education and catechesis of adolescents?

If we are astonished at their attitudes of moral relativism, desire for independence, frenzy for life and sensation, we must also be able to diagnose, along with all that is wrong, a reaction against suffocation and an overflow of spiritual vitality. This has momentous consequences for morality.

When carried to the extreme, we have here a moral sense (like that of Sartre and Françoise Sagan) in which subjectivity is all that matters. Individual freedom sets up its own norms and creates its own value system: Truth is whatever agrees with my love for life. Happiness is emotional equilibrium—feeling well, being in harmony with myself. Being a worthwhile person means possessing myself through living every moment in its fullness and respecting everyone else's right to do so. To live, says Françoise Sagan, "is to make sure that you are as satisfied as possible."

Everything is here defined in terms of vital exuberance and freedom—but a freedom and exuberance lived in utter human loneliness. Sartre wrote quite rightly: "A man who is without love, without family or home is no longer free. Or rather, he has the freedom of those filaments which the wind tears from spider webs and which float through the air a few feet above the ground."[21]

Few young people, of course, would explicitly adhere to such a morality. It is beyond human possibility because of the rigor of its nihilism, but it pervades the air they breathe.[22]

What are the repercussions of this thirst for life in the light of faith? This excessive instinctivity should not frighten us or make us desperate. What matters is that we know how to understand and interpret the "call" of the instincts— on the one hand its helplessness and deviation, on the other its great thirst. Our faith and love must be strong enough to enable us to make genuine contact with these powerful cries that rise from the earth. Only then can we make them open to the Kingdom of God.

Why should the frenzy of Rock 'n Roll throw men into a panic who experience daily the springing forth of the Living Water in personal contact with the Lord of Life and

[21] *The Flies.*

[22] P., a sophomore in high school, wrote in large letters on the cover of his notebooks: "Love is egoism between two people."—"If you feel like working lie down on your bed until you're over it!"— "One is loneliest in one's family."

Glory? Jesus would say to us: "Why are you fearful, men of little faith?"

Moreover, we know that this hunger for life, if channeled and "assumed,"[23] is the will of the Lord. It is an opportunity for the young generation to become more lucid, vigorous, and hence more fully human in its allegiance to Christ, who would make of us His own Body. After today's adolescents have passed through the turbulence of their instincts they will be able to offer the entire earth to the Lord. The man who, from his youth, has retained the ability to savor human values, material realities, and earthly tasks is more particularly called to achieve the world's consecration to God.

This is no doubt the first reason why the thought of P. Teilhard de Chardin arouses such enthusiasm among young people. He is a symbol for them because he knows how to link a cosmic view of the world with the concrete realism of scientific work. For him human realities can also be the glory of God.

Here is the enthusiastic testimony of a young college student, who cites at length Teilhard de Chardin's hymn to the Church in The Divine Milieu:

"Jerusalem, lift up your head. Look at the immense crowds of those who build and those who seek. All over the world, men are toiling—in laboratories, in studios, in deserts, in factories, in the vast social crucible. The ferment that is taking place by their instrumentality in art and science and thought is happening for your sake. Open, then, your arms and your heart, like Christ your Lord, and welcome the

[23] Assumed: literally, "taking upon oneself."—Trans.

waters, the flood and the sap of humanity. Accept it, this sap,—for, without its baptism, you will wither, without desire, like a flower out of water; and tend it, since, without your sun, it will disperse itself wildly in sterile shoots."[24]

Dazzled by this vision the young student adds: "At times I am exhausted by all this. It is so powerful! His language is at once so concrete and so abstract! I can't sit still any more. I feel as if I were caught up by a power that shakes me, that my own person is no longer big enough to contain this intoxicating force."

We must not be naïve, however. Such lyrical accents are not only rare but also ambiguous. We know that there is often a great gap between grandiose dreams and the humble faith of the Church of Christ. We find here once again the great danger of instinctual exuberance,[25] not so much, perhaps, in sexual indulgence as in subjective imprisonment in the cult of sensation and in an attitude of self-sufficiency. The Gospel always meets its greatest enemies in the Pharisees and Sadducees.

The Adolescents' Progressive Socialization

Let us briefly consider one last characteristic: the trend toward socialization in today's youth. By "socialization" we mean the progressive relinquishing of their individual characteristics as unique persons in favor of standardization and of action in and by the group.

[24] Pierre Teilhard de Chardin, S.J., *The Divine Milieu* (New York: Harper, 1960), p. 138.
[25] See above, "The Act of Faith and the Adolescent," pp. 23 ff.

Socialization is in the first place a defense mechanism against an out-of-date society and modern institutions that are de-personalizing because they are cold and anonymous. If we question the truth of this statement, let us observe young people in situations where they can really be themselves. They generally refuse to let themselves be buried in big youth organizations. Instead, they form small groups with only a few members, where they can feel at home. They reject rules imposed from without but readily accept regulations of small groups which they have joined of their own accord—athletic clubs, discussion groups, etc., where they can be themselves in a relaxed atmosphere and common creative action. In such a climate the human person can be fully himself, find himself as "I" in relationship to a "Thou." It is not surprising to note, therefore, that groups based on social pressure or geographical proximity (i.e., attending the same school or parish) are often less tightly knit than freely chosen groups. This is important to remember for those responsible for the guidance of young people and youth groups. If these groups are to meet the aspirations of today's youth, we must ensure for them an authentically human quality which will permit personal relationships among individual members.[26]

This socialization expresses, furthermore, a basic demand

[26] Before they are thrown into activity adolescents need to form relationships. On the Christian plane we have sufficiently pointed out that an activity which does not have its roots in a true human and spiritual community will die before long. Apostolic education has insisted strongly on "things to be done," on having an influence, etc. It seems to us that it is important to put greater emphasis today on the quality of our relationships—not through human instinctivity, but by sharing in the movement of the infinite Charity of God.

of our modern technological world, the desire for achievement. Men of primitive societies were forced to live together in order to feel safe against the forces of nature. Modern men are still driven together to confront these forces—not, however, in order to protect themselves as in former times, but to bring them under control and make them serve scientific progress. If young people today want to live together, travel, and be in touch with other worlds, they do so because they want to know a greater dimension of reality and make a better life for themselves.

Among the consequences of socialization, we find that individual characteristics are gradually levelled off, while the interaction of persons becomes more pronounced and conditions their entire moral conduct and way of life.

The key words now are: community, influence, public relations, job, understanding, commitment. The values of interiority are measured by the quality of action and relationships. In the words of Ricœur, "What you do is a pledge of what you are." By the same token the values of individuality in and for itself become less important than interpersonal values.[27] Thus the human person is in danger of becoming standardized, and those of exceptional talent retreat before the mediocre average. However, this is in no way to deny the existence of small closed groups, which allow for individual expression.

[27] Much could be done in this respect to orientate adolescents toward acquiring not only an autonomous personality, but a social personality, capable of genuine relationships, of specific action and influence in and through a group. This should also inform our catechesis on the Church in the sense of making young people aware of their own vocation in and for the Kingdom of God.

Moral values will be greatly influenced by group opinion and taste. Anyone who withdraws from the demands of the group and falls back on his individual decision is labeled a coward. "Today's youth tends toward a community morality," writes Jousselin. "That is to say, it is dominated not so much by the notion of truth as by the idea of loyalty, if we take this term in its primary meaning of 'fidelity.' It is essentially a question of a morality of belonging to a determined human group, whose demands constitute one of the primary elements in establishing right and wrong."[28] We see this carried to the extreme in a peculiar gang morality, which takes pride in stealing from store counters, or attacking women.

In this perspective hero worship is replaced by worship of the gang or group. The adolescent's choices are determined by the group to which he belongs, rather than by a personal hero or ideal.

One adolescent commented that on the mountain tops nowadays crosses have been replaced by radar and TV antennae. A sign of the times! In the clear light of faith, however, are not the mass communication media a touchstone of that far more profound communion "of another world" to which Christ still calls men by His Cross and

---

[28] Jousselin, *Jeunesse, phénomène social*, p. 21.—Jean Daniélou, S.J., in *Études* (January, 1960), expresses the same reality: "More importance is attached to the sincerity with which man lives his faith than to the objective value of that faith. . . . In place of the idea of an objective morality, which is conforming one's actions to the will of God, there is substituted an individual ethic which is conformity of one's actions with one's own view of things. . . . One's only duty is to go to the limits of oneself, whether it be in the will to power, in revolutionary action, or in the night of contemplation."

Resurrection?[29] Does not human socialization find its ful-fillment in the Good News of true brotherhood in Christ?

Many young people are aware of the world's progress toward unity. They are ready to leave behind sterile quarrels and narrow prejudices, and to think in terms of large crowds and vast masses.[30] In place of abstract discussion they believe in the effectiveness of work and power of human endeavor, and in interpersonal understanding. With earnestness and realism they want to build a better world, where men can live in unity and brotherhood.

Surely this is a privileged hour for the Church!

Moreover, the best among them are not satisfied with a merely geographic unity, however vast. They want unity that is profoundly communal. Let us recall here the small cell groups, apostolic teams, various clubs, and even sects.[31]

If given an evangelical formation, young people will gradually find again the strength, intensity and vitality of those early Christian communities which the Acts of the Apostles describe with such joy.

Some sociologists today speak of a "silent revolution" with reference to the profound but confused evolution of today's youth.

If we have accurately assessed the historical importance

[29] Cf. Cardinal Suhard, *Growth or Decline?*

[30] We may never forget, however, that beyond this more general current there are some strong and active minorities that tend toward a neonationalism, through fear, reaction, or simply instinct. These minorities will be the more active as they become more crystallized in anger against political inaction or weakness. Not a few disillu-sioned young people are ready to support a dictatorship or fascism.

[31] Cf. Brien, "Les petites communautés, soutiens de la foi," in *Études* (November, 1953).

of their numerical growth, and the dimension of the new mentality developing among them, the word "revolution" is indeed none too strong.

Will all this human newness, this wealth trying to find itself, achieve its full growth in truth and depth through consecration to Jesus Christ?

PART TWO

EDUCATORS FOR TODAY'S YOUTH

CHAPTER FIVE

CONDITIONS FOR A CHRISTIAN EDUCATION

We might be tempted to answer the questions raised by the psychological analysis of adolescents and their crisis of faith with quick, easy solutions. In discussing the problems of their growing children with the teacher, parents often ask for systems, for pat answers which might help them—as though all that were needed is a magic wand. In fact, something quite different from mere words is called for here.

Being, rather than doing, counts at this time. The old adage, "You accomplish more by what you are than by what you say, or even by what you do," is particularly applicable in adolescence.[1] We must surround the young person with an atmosphere of personal bonds between adults and adolescents, and among adolescents themselves. Education at this time may be said to be "atmospheric."

This importance of the atmosphere and relationships surrounding him arises from his psychological situation. The adolescent is straining with his whole self toward his adult equilibrium. A new and personal being that desires auton-

[1] Also in childhood, which resembles adolescence in many ways.

omy and self-confidence is trying to find itself in him. His first psychological need, then, is that we rejoin him at this primitive level where he is still undifferentiated. Tomorrow, as an adult, he will be like a river whose banks and currents are clearly outlined; today he resembles a spring that bubbles and tries to find an outlet. Like the young child in his first blossoming, the adolescent must be touched in the depths of his being, where he exists essentially as drive, dynamism, search, and restlessness.

A teacher of youth is one who knows how to educate the person's emotional life, and not merely the orientation of his will. Many times we can achieve more through suggestions, a smile, or moments of silence than through sharp orders.

A teacher of youth is one who knows how to educate the person not merely on the conscious level, but in that psychological state where the faculties are still insufficiently differentiated. Often a favorable atmosphere, a shared action or common experience, will have more effect than a clear, precise explanation.

A teacher of youth is one who knows how to educate the person in his painful, groping quest—not merely his rational faculty. Often a comforting presence, a friendly remark, or an inductive intellectual process will achieve more than the demonstration of a thesis.

A teacher of youth is one who knows how to educate the person to see things in terms of their purpose and meaning, rather than function. Often a fact, attitude, or symbol will answer their genuine questions better than a theory.

What do adolescents expect of us today? We have no intention of indulging in anti-intellectualism. Objective and precise knowledge is necessary because we must educate not only for today but for tomorrow. Both the Church and society require this of us, and their needs are primary in education. We shall single out here only the main points, in the light of the psychological data as it applies to the adolescent's intellect and affective life.

Tomorrow, as an adult, he will be more easily satisfied with precise, objective, even impersonal knowledge and with a value synthesis. Today, as adolescent, he very badly needs a friendly, reliable presence, a wise teacher whose way of life can inspire him and exert an influence. We shall try to answer two questions in this chapter:

1) Young people want to be understood. What does this mean?

2) They are not satisfied with words. What "event," what witness do they expect of us?

Education Through Understanding

In all the studies we were able to make, *the* quality required of teachers by adolescents is understanding.[2] This is listed ahead of all others and described in different words which clarify its meaning:

Girls:

understanding, openmindedness	62%
youthful, relaxed appearance	59%
dedication, friendliness	56%

[2] P. Babin, "What youth thinks of priests and the religious life." *Lumen Vitae*, VIII, 1953, No. 4, pp. 639 ff.

Boys:
friendliness, understanding, dedication 54%
flexibility 24%

In other studies, where the synonyms of the word "understanding" were combined, a percentage of 80% was obtained.

"Sometimes I think that grown-ups have quite forgotten that they were young once because they don't understand us at all," writes an adolescent girl. What is the meaning of this magic word, "understanding"? At a time when the gap between the generations becomes wider and when a feeling of fear, even of failure, haunts educators, it is more necessary than ever to consider the conditions that make possible genuine understanding.

The young people themselves sound the alarm, but we must not expect of them genuine insight into their situation. There is nothing worse than a Machiavellian understanding. Nor is there anything worse than the teacher who, devoid of character and personality, is obsessed with adapting himself so as to be a success. It is not a question of success as teacher, but of serving the success of human freedom. To clarify this let us examine both the natural and supernatural meanings of understanding.

By "understanding" we do not mean "indulgence." Contemporary history has taught us that the release of all restrictions produces sadists and criminals. On the other hand, we must avoid blanket restrictions which inhibit spontaneity. Such an atmosphere produces resentment, people ridden with complexes, the immature adults so prevalent in our society.

Let us consider a situation that might well occur today: Peter, age 16, comes to see one of his teachers and brings him a record. "You spoke in class the other day of the Industrial Revolution in Russia. Have you heard this record about the steel works there?" They look at each other. Peter gives him the record. He puts it on and plays one side as they both listen. Timidly, Peter waits for his teacher's enthusiastic comment. . . . "Yes, it surely evokes overtones of the power of the revolutionary movement, the power of man and machines." Thereupon Peter pulls a piece of paper from his pocket: "Here, I wrote down a few thoughts . . . It's all about man's fate and history, things all the boys are wondering about."

The teacher reads. Peter, a bit worried, watches for his least reaction. The silence is rather strained. It is impossible for the teacher to say that everything Peter had written was good in every respect! When he has finished reading he says: "You have tackled a difficult subject, Peter. It's a good thing that you're concerned about this. This particular passage is excellent; here I don't quite see it the way you do. . . . But it is good that you raise this question here. We'll talk some more about it."

Then suddenly Peter asks: "What do you think of young people? Do you think they're all right?" The teacher nods, and Peter continues: "Because my parents are always telling me that we're second-rate. But I'm sure we'll amount to something, someday."

This summary of a conversation shows clearly what the

adolescent needs if he is to be understood. A theory on the Soviet experiment? A thesis on man's fate? If the teacher had expounded learnedly on Soviet man he would never have set eyes on what Peter had written. If he had philosophized objectively on fate, Peter would never have asked him the question about young people and—this is far more serious—he would not have helped Peter grow up.

What the adolescent wants *first of all* is a positive Yes from his teacher, the friendship of a man with prestige who shares his quest and secret hopes. Once this has been given and assured there will be time for more objective explanations. With progressive intellectual explanations Peter's whole person will be strengthened, educated, and inspired to go beyond itself.

The psychologist Carl Rogers expresses[3] very well the true meaning of education through understanding:

> If, in my encounter with the other, I treat him as a child, an ignorant student, a neurotic or psychopath, each of my conceptions will limit what he might be able to say to me. . . . Martin Buber . . . has a phrase, "confirming the other," which has had meaning for me. He says confirming means . . . accepting the whole potentiality of the other. . . . I recognize in him, know in him, the person he has been . . . created to become. . . . I confirm him in myself, and then in him, in relation to this potentiality that . . . can now be developed, can evolve. If I accept the other person as something fixed, already diagnosed and classified, already shaped by his past, then I am doing my part to confirm this limited hypothesis. If I accept him as a process of becoming, then I am doing what I can to confirm or make real his potentialities. . . .
>
> If I see relationship as only opportunity to reinforce certain

[3] Carl Rogers, in *Personnel and Guidance Journal*, Vol. 37, No. 1 (September 1958), pp. 6–16.

types of words or opinions in the other, then I tend to confirm him as an object—a basically mechanical, manipulable object. And if I see this as his potentiality, he tends to act in ways which support this hypothesis. If on the other hand I see a relationship as an opportunity to "reinforce" all that he is, the person that he is with all his existent potentialities, then he tends to act in ways which support this hypothesis. I have then —to use Buber's terms—confirmed him as a living person capable of creative inner development.

What are the elements of education through understanding? Understanding someone is not in the first place a technique, or a bit of facile knowledge, something that you do or don't do. Understanding someone is above all striving for a certain outlook, a presence and relationship. It is a mixture of humility and awareness, friendship and trust, silence and absolute hope in the other.

All the psychology books, studies and tests, will not help us to understand the adolescent if we do not attain this spiritual outlook. To understand is to "stand under," i.e., to support. It is to set out with the other in a common direction, to accompany him.

In Rogers' words we might say: to understand is to listen so intently that we confirm the other's potentialities through the quality of the relationship we establish with him.

1) To understand is first to discover the potentialities of the other, that secret place where all that is best in him, all that can be perfected, resides. Take Jim, for example—lazy and rebellious. It is impossible to get him to study; but he does well in drawing and design. One day a teacher enters his life who recognizes this, recognizes him in that

point which is his talent for drawing. The teacher makes
contact with him through this point, makes him work, and
gradually lifts him above his rebellion and laziness. "You
will become a man through your artistic work. I recognize
you in this, in all that you can create, and I call you through
this precise point of yourself."

It goes without saying that such perceptiveness requires
great spiritual poverty, detachment from self, in order to be
free for the other. In this sense, "the opposite of a true
teacher of youth is the self-made man, the man sure of himself, who dazzles others with his own experience and contacts; the Pharisee who is perhaps conscientious, precise and
strong, but rich only with himself. And Pharisaism is without the shadow of a doubt the biggest force of education
for all time! Adolescents feel this when they instinctively
prefer to the teacher who is 'master of himself and the
world' a man who occasionally loses his temper, but who
remains small and humble, continues to seek and mount up-
ward."[4]

2) To understand is to have a *deeper vision of the other's
potentialities.* For the Christian this vision is located at two
levels. First, *natural knowledge:* thanks to his experience,
knowledge, and skill the teacher has in principle a deeper,
more extensive knowledge of the adolescent's talents or
possibilities. He knows that drawing can help make him a
man because it permits him to express himself, to com-
municate with others and to create. Second, *the knowledge*

[4] Congress held at Angers, 1958, "Pastorale de l'adolescence," p.
132.

of faith: the Christian teacher knows this talent even more deeply in God. He knows that, through artisic creation, man can become to an ever higher degree a son of God; he knows that this sonship grows by being purified, and that through it he will draw his brothers into the world of spiritual realities. Jim made great progress from the day he was given charge of the bulletin board and the school's liturgical display.

3) To understand is *to confirm the potentialities of the other through the genuineness of our friendship and weight of our prestige.* Life is communicated in interpersonal relationships. If we have joined the adolescent in his humble quest, he will feel reassured and spurred on to other adventures, for one value calls forth other values. Thanks to the self-confidence which he acquired through his drawing, Jim now has the courage to study English and mathematics.

4) To understand is *to confirm the other through our teaching,* by helping him become a better person and develop what is now present only in germ. To join another in his unique manner of being able to love and create—to awaken him and confirm him in that point where all that is best in him resides—this is the meaning of "education through understanding."

It should go without saying that detachment from self is a pre-requisite for understanding. Let us again take a typical example. A mother complains to the teacher that she no longer understands her son. "Until now I was able to follow him more or less, but for some time now it's been hopeless. For instance, we used to sit and talk together after dinner, so as to keep the family together. But now that he's grown up and we have TV, he no longer wants to talk. The moment we've finished eating he runs to the TV set. I don't know what to do. Our family life is breaking up."

What is happening here? Let us listen to the adolescent: "My mother doesn't understand a thing! There's nothing wrong with watching TV!" Of course there is nothing wrong with it. But what is still more certain is that there is no understanding on either side. Each goes his own way.

What is to be done? The solution could come from the child if he submits to his mother's viewpoint; or it could come from the mother if she adapts herself to his. Which of the two will make the first step to cross the gap, so that they can find each other again?

We are of the opinion that, generally speaking, it is up to parents and teachers throughout the entire period of adolescence to make the first step. Not, certainly, in order to "support" evil—evil cannot be supported—but in order to support in the adolescent all that is *possible*, all his potentialities, even if they are very different from our own ideas.[5]

During childhood the parents had imposed on him their own ideas about life and relationships. This was normal enough, and adapted to the needs of the child. Today, however, he must leave childhood behind if he is to become an adult, a person who has his own vocation and way of living—a vocation in line with a unique impulse of creation.

---

[5] We are suggesting here a general orientation, a climate rather than a law. In actual practice we should be flexible. The father who comes home at night tired out from his job should not feel obliged, under pretext of understanding, to put up with the noise of Rock 'n Roll which his son likes to play without interruption!

The teacher should courageously lay aside imposing his own way of living on the adolescent.

If he succeeds in stripping himself of his own will, in detaching himself from his way of doing and feeling, he will then be able to recognize the other's possibilities and ineffectual drives. He will be able to stand close to this young person who is trying to fly from the nest and be himself in all his uniqueness. He will say to him: "Go ahead, my friend! I say to you with the full weight of my being, of my love and my experience—Go ahead!"

To understand is not to want another to become my own image and likeness. It is to leave myself behind and seek, not my own reflection, but another person who is different and unique in the splendor and variety of his eternal vocation.

Young people today love TV. This is a fact, and it is not in itself an evil. Someone should explain to the mother that TV is an asset as well as a risk. She should be made to see that instead of being angry, she must be willing to give up her own ideas and certain forms of family life. Then she will surely succeed in restoring, thanks to that very TV, the family spirit which rightly means so much to her. Was not this Pius XII's thought when he described TV as a means of avoiding the break-up of the family and tightening the family bond? Is not this what God does when He understands us? God's greatest joy is to create a free human being—to call into existence an original creator, face-to-face with Himself, who can enter into dialogue and encounter with Him.

God's supreme greatness is to love and passionately desire

the freedom of man—not a man asleep, who mumbles a passive "Amen," but one who is awake, alive, responsible, who weeps, loves, and creates.

To understand is to share in God's infinite desire to create freedom, a desire which went so far as the Incarnation and Redemption. On that day God definitively realized His "plan of understanding." Man was at last involved with God in a free, eternal Covenant of salvation.

Let us consider what this means in terms of the sanctity of the teacher. Young people are not fooled: to understand them requires great faith and great love. There are certain types of instinctive, superficial understanding which do not last. True understanding consists of silence, of cherishing God's will in men. It is built up through sharing in Jesus' unique manner of seeing each person and calling him by name. It culminates in a faithful alertness to the other, in humble service that does not shrink back even from the Cross.

Young people today have a special need of such understanding because they are so insecure in this new, topsy-turvy world. Who will help them to mature, to make their own the new values trying to take shape in their hearts? Who but the educator whose faith in the Lord's power is so great that his faith in them cannot be shaken?

We cannot educate if we no longer believe in the other. . . . Does not hell consist precisely in this—that man's drive to freedom tears him out of God's love? God can no longer believe in him . . .

What cannot be understood, and what can always be understood? Let us be clear about it: there is one thing which we may never "support" and which must make us weep—that is, sin. Sin, said Claudel, is precisely "that which does not exist." If we see in the sinner a marvelous possibility in the order of Redemption, we do not admit sin as such and we must make it clear that his sin hurts us. For sin does not make the greatness of man but undoes it. Everything else the teacher must take unto himself, as Christ did in His redemptive Incarnation.

To sum up: Christian understanding has as its object all that is richest and most dangerous in another person, the drive of his freedom, the unique orientation of his will.[6] A young person will always feel himself understood if we desire, with our full adult being, all the grandeur of his freedom—ultimately, his vocation.

Education Through Witness

The teacher's witness must be a "love-event." Words by themselves are not enough. Françoise Sagan said in an interview: "People scare me who want to change you at all costs. We are what we are and that is as it should be. I can easily imagine someone I love or some event changing my life. But to change myself, radically, deep down, no. . . . Until now there have been three decisive events in my life: the success of my books, the famous accident, and my marriage."

---

[6] This includes, in the concrete, his sensibility, his way of facing reality, of desiring, of loving. We might speak of free will as an adventurous spirit; of freedom, on the other hand (in the manner of St. Augustine) as man's impulse, unhampered, going toward the good.

These words typify very well her point of view, namely, a total refusal to listen to people who, no matter how sincere and convinced they may be, try to reach her from the outside; the impossibility of changing herself from within, because she has decided to be a law unto herself; finally, the only things that can change her life are facts or events insofar as they are inescapable realities—and on the other hand, love, as a reality which reaches her in her "I" and tears her from herself.

Theories, words, empty chatter—young people want none of this; partly, no doubt, because their generation is used to dealing with things objectively, but even more because they have been too often deceived and pushed around.[7]

We must insist on this last point. We have no right to judge the young man who says, "There is nothing but getting drunk," or, "We are what we are." We must respect his view. It is surely because he has too often been left in the lurch that he can believe only in what he touches and in what he is.

How can words reach the young person who is alone, whom no human presence surrounds, who experiences a broken home or simply the psychological absence of parents imprisoned in their worries, work, and problems? Words, in such circumstances, are nothing but derision or pretext for

[7] "One of the most characteristic aspects of our era is our mistrust of words. . . . Men of today, because they have been deceived, no longer trust in words. Every statement is suspect. . . . Big words have camouflaged the worst kinds of propaganda. . . . Today's youth, instead of clinging to big words emptied of their content, adheres to the concrete realities of their private life, of scientific equipment, of economic research."—Jean Daniélou, S.J., in *Études* (January 1960), p. 5.

revolt. The only escape from the frustration and boredom of existence is fast living, excitement, sex, etc.

People who have been deceived, left alone or crushed can believe neither in words, ideas, nor exhortations. This insecure but realistic generation wants facts, events—but what sort of facts? What event? Not only small concrete witness, however live it may be, but that absolute, visible, certain Fact and Event: Jesus Christ alive today.

And why Jesus Christ? Because Jesus Christ is the one Fact from which one cannot escape. He is the Event of Love. Through faith we know this fact which young people await, from which they cannot escape: the Church in their lives, the continuation of the Incarnation.[8]

We do not mean, of course, the Church in the abstract, nor the building of stone that happens to be in their part of town, but the true Church, living and whole, in which Christ's love continues on. In this Church the Lord of Glory ceases not to enter tangibly into a relationship of love with modern man, to his undoing or his salvation. This fact cannot be manifested by one individual alone, or by the exposition of a theory. It is essentially a *relationship*.

The Christian event which they await is always the same. It is the Love-event in all its aspects: a love that is tangible, communal, and fraternal (Incarnation); a love that suffers

[8] The effort of so many youth chaplains to join their young people on the level of the "facts of life" is symptomatic. This pedagogy, which is so necessary today, is not first of all the concern to be concrete, but the desire to share young people's lives, their questions, work, circumstances, i.e., all that is close to them. The pedagogy of the "facts of life" is the education of the Incarnation, the act through which God joins the "fact" of man's life in order to make of it the "fact" of His own Life.

and forgives (Easter, the Pasch); a love that reaches into infinity (Pentecost).

As educators we should pronounce words only if there is real love in our hearts. We should use words only when we are in the "state of grace," that is, under the compelling impulse of Jesus Christ's infinite generosity. Otherwise this generation will find our comedy unbearable. We shall be held responsible for "quenching the smoking wick." In the light of modern man's expectation, woe to the teacher who does not live what he teaches and does not love with the charity of that God whom he pretends to proclaim!

The leaders of this time, from Nietzsche to Sartre, have too often echoed Christ's anathemas against the Pharisees, hypocrites, and the self-satisfied to permit us to continue "teaching in the chair of Moses" if our lives are discordant, commonplace, and banal.

We must describe in more detail the nuances of this Love-event which they expect from us.

Love is an encounter and dialogue with the other. In order to achieve a truer and more profound encounter the teacher will seek to meet the concrete expectations of young people, according to the fullness and truth of Jesus Christ. They thirst for freedom, exuberance, and the joy of living. Our charity, then, must be permeated with freedom, youthfulness, and joy, if it is ever to reach them. How is this possible when so many teachers are weighted down with years, work, and care? And, quite simply, how is this possible for us "poor sinners?"

Freedom is a fundamental question of today's youth. What novel does not speak of it? Where is the teacher who does not have to deal with this problem among crowds of girls and boys who ask all sorts of impossible questions? All too often the Christian, the teacher, or the educational system itself witnesses to a life that is narrow, undernourished, and depersonalized.[9]

Over and above theoretical explanations young people must recognize in the Church the witness of true freedom. Let their teachers really appear free, that is, let them live their commitment to God passionately and without regret.

In the Church of their teachers young people must discover that obedience to Jesus Christ makes men free. It is not facile rebellion on our part against authority and certain aspects of the Church that will give them the experience of freedom, but rather the fact that a Christian, in obedience, achieves his own holiness, becomes someone who loves and creates values in a climate of love and joy.

To be free, young people say, is to do whatever you want. They must come to see that in the Church you do what you want, in the sense that, for a Christian, "to want" is to participate with one's entire humanity in the infinite vitality and freedom of God.

Young people soon learn that the independence of the

[9] P. Babin, op. cit., p. 651. Speaking of nuns, the girls said: "I would like her not to be enclosed, but in contact with life and, consequently, knowing life, broader in her ideas." Without going as far as one girl, who affirmed that "the essence of religious life is to have no initiative," many believe that obedience destroys initiative. "I would like her not to be a coward before her superior but enterprising, full of initiative." "She should remain as human as possible." They do not want their nuns to be "too virtuous," shut in, but "nuns who are lively, smiling, gay and young (79% of the 14–15 year olds), showing that religious life does not stifle spontaneity, human values, above all, joy.

"Christian on vacation" does not lead to the unfolding of true freedom. What they need to find in Christian communities is the radiance of a positive freedom; not one which measures itself in terms of phantasy or dissipation, but of creation and love. A person will appear free in the measure in which he hopes, gives, and loves greatly. Is not this the freedom which the Lord gives?

It is important that the teacher be youthful. It is a well-known fact that young people make fun of the adult's age. Confronted by the world of adults who appear far removed from them, adolescents proclaim a sharp break and vigorously flaunt their youth. They are the ones who are going ahead, while behind them totter the old folks who know nothing of life.

Wise parents and educators know very well that they will be able to reach their children only if they themselves remain young.

In teaching children, one can remain attached to the ways of one's own childhood. While this is not ideal it may be valid, for the child finds his equilibrium within his parents' world. To educate an adolescent, on the other hand, is to help make a person whose equilibrium will rest not on us, but within himself, in the midst of the world, outside of us. Hence there can be no question of keeping our eyes riveted on our past.

But, is it really possible to remain youthful? In order to remain young some people pursue sports; others methodically practice physical culture. Still others try to keep close to teenagers. All this is well and good. But is it really possible to remain close to young people and not grow old in our way of educating? How can the teacher maintain the joy and youthful enthusiasm indispensable to his influence? There are, in fact, three kinds of youthfulness. The first, physical youth, consists of a certain bodily vigor which urges us to conquer rather than protect, advance rather than retreat, dare rather than be secure, adapt rather than reject. Here, the vitality is greater than the need to conserve and preserve, and one does not even count the cost of what one gives. "My life at its dawn," writes Tagore, "resembled a flower, an open flower which loses a petal or two from her abundance and never feels the loss when the breeze of spring comes knocking at her door. Today at the end of my youth, my life is like a fruit which has nothing left to spare: it only waits to offer itself completely with its full burden of sweetness."[10]

Then there is intellectual youth, which seems to consist essentially of a certain curiosity which keeps asking questions, which is surprised with wonder and sympathetically understands all that is, no matter how new. It makes possible the adaptation to new situations, not through reference to previous ones, but through an objective consideration of the actual problem at hand. When we have become old-fashioned, worn out by life, when we can no longer stand changes and classify problems by saying, "When I was young . . ."—then we have lost intellectual youth.

The last is spiritual youth. The youth of the body fades and passes away like the grass of the fields, the Bible tells us. The youth of the intellect will sooner or later share the

[10] Rabindranath Tagore, *Fruit Gathering* (New York: Macmillan, 1916).

same fate, because man is limited in his ability to absorb
the world and to create. The youth of the spirit, however, is
eternal because it is of another world, the world of charity.

General MacArthur felt this when he wrote, in words
which come close to an explicitly Christian perspective:
"He is young who can still be surprised, who asks, 'And
then?' like a child that always wants more. He takes life as
it comes and enjoys every moment of it.

"You are as young as your faith, as old as your doubt,
young as your confidence in yourself, young as your hope,
old as your despair.

"You will remain young as long as you remain open to
what is beautiful, good and great, open to the message of
nature, of man and the infinite."

In the perspective of faith spiritual youth is the opposite
of self-sufficiency. It is not possession of life, not even possession of a virtuous life, but rather, joyful poverty and an
ever greater openness to God's infinite, vital dynamism. It
demands of us that we give up trying to make a success of
our life through our own physical resources and the modern
techniques for remaining young, which are geared toward
social success and self-development.

He is truly young who radically entrusts his life to the
autonomy, freedom, and vital dynamism which the heavenly Father gives to men in His Son Jesus.

For a teacher, only this spiritual youth can be the basis
for a profound, abiding understanding of young people that
lies beyond the inevitable process of aging of our physical
and intellectual powers. Why? Because such youthfulness

is the fruit of a knowledge and charity that do not fade—because they are of God.

Such knowledge is not simply the product of intellectual vigor, but above all the fruit of the Holy Spirit who, as Christ promised, introduces us day by day a little more deeply into all truth. It participates therefore in the characteristics of divine knowledge, which is infinitely young and all-inclusive. This knowledge is not static, fixed, or abstract. It goes to the heart of man in order to discern there all his possibilities and cause the seed of eternity to awaken. It is a knowledge which desires, calls, and waits for the other, in the sureness of hope. An adolescent whom we know in this way trembles with joy and experiences a new birth. How could he call "old" one who dares look at him with such depth and confidence?

An old teacher who had been enchantingly beautiful in her youth once told us: "God has made me understand. Now I am becoming poorer and poorer. I no longer look for physical beauty in the girls nor for expressions of their love, but only for one thing: their vocation, their grace." This teacher had remained truly young through her unshakeable faith in the other, by being stripped of herself, and breaking through the closed circle of her own life.

The old man who has remained youthful has depth and hope in his eyes. Detached from nonessentials, from "worldly goods" which pass away, he sees reality with the eyes of the Kingdom of God, and his hope in man, and in man's eternal vocation is a foretaste of the Resurrection.

Spiritual youth, then, is *faith* and *hope*; it is also, essentially, charity. Through charity the teacher opens his whole being more and more to a profound attentiveness to the other, a warm, all-inclusive sympathy, to a service of his brothers that is ever more humble, and generous to the point of sacrifice.

It is God's will that we possess youth at all three levels as long as possible. We must understand clearly, however, that it is for spiritual youth that we should strive with all the passion of our heart.[11] And it is this supernatural youth which will determine the youthfulnss of body and intellect, insofar as this is possible.

Furthermore, it is the Church who is the sign of the Lord's eternal youth in this world. Let us not monopolize eternal youth for any one stage in man's life. It is the community, not an individual, that will sound the authentic ring of youth, into which blend the shades and qualities of all the ages of man.

Adolescents, more than children, need teachers who have a certain physical and intellectual youth; they should have such teachers. But it would also be well if they had others whose only youth is that of faith and charity. How great will be their impact!

[11] Whereas true youth consists in the gift of self to others, a false youth consists essentially in the cult of self, which can verge on the idolatry of physical culture or the more subtle error of a false angelism and spiritualization of the body. Jesus expressed this succinctly: "He who would save his life [His breath, the vital principal of the first Adam] shall lose it. He who loses his life will save it." In this context it is quite normal that the educator, as he grows older, will leave behind certain forms of presence and of educational method which characterized him during his physical youth. He will instead take on forms more stripped of self, in which there is a greater spirit of service: passing from friendship to a fatherly presence.

It is the community that is the repository of the infinitely varied youthfulness of God.

Then there is joy. Do Christians today give the witness of peace and joy? One boy told his teacher, who was doing a study on his students' mentality: "Don't think that we want to be like our parents. No, we don't. My father is always telling me: 'You should be an engineer' . . . To live the way he does—No thanks!"

Such remarks are not rare even among children of good Christian families. They express disillusionment, but even more deeply frustration in their affective life.

The spectacle of adults does not always make one want to be like them. Not so much, perhaps, because they are lacking in virtue, but because they are empty of happiness. To hear young people talk often makes you feel that their parents have not given them any joy of living; and so they must seek this joy elsewhere. Happiness is the great force of this century. All the magazines, movies, and songs make us dream of it; but, we may ask, have Christians borne witness to it?

Young people too often have the impression that you cannot at the same time be virtuous and happy, fully Christian and fully human. "Don't talk to me about my parents," said a nineteen-year-old girl. "I can't stand that kind of people any more. My mother is in Catholic Action, she is a woman of duty. My father is a lawyer, he is a man of principle! Women of duty and men of principle—you can have them!"

Complaining of this rather general state of affairs, a journalist quoted someone who felt himself caught in this false dilemma between Christianity and death, or world and happiness: "On the one hand, there are the dehydrated Christians, excessively stiff, faithless to their humanity, people who are hardened in servile observance of empty practices. . . . On the other, there are those who thirst for life, men with rich possibilities and vast desires, who want to develop the whole man. The former call them 'pagans.' "

In professional life the same thing frequently holds true: adults do not link joy with work, a full humanity with their profession. It is true that circumstances are often difficult, even inhuman, and that the sudden invasion of modern technology creates acute imbalance. And yet we may ask: Is it normal to see adults weighed down as though the burden of the world were on their shoulders?

Such criticism is serious and quite common. It testifies to a crisis among parents as well as adolescents.[12]

Where are the responsibilities for this situation to be placed? It is certainly not a matter of blaming Catholic Action, which tries precisely to link the temporal with the spiritual. The situation is not entirely of our own doing. It partly stems from the sudden invasion of a traditional outlook and way of life by the modern industrial world. It is due, also, to a sudden, often tragic awakening to the de-Christianization of the masses, the urgency of the missionary question, underdeveloped countries, etc.

We may ask, however, whether this is not also our sin.

---

[12] Cf. "Journées nationales de l'Enseignement Religieux" (Paris, 1959). Surveys made in different dioceses throughout France showed that many parents engaged in the apostolate have serious fears that they have failed in the education of their adolescent sons and daughters.

Do we not need to denounce vigorously, among many Christians who claim to be fervent, a certain activism and tension which stamp their spiritual life with pessimism and Pelagianism? "My parents are dreadful," says one youngster. "Whenever they have seen someone they keep wondering how he reacted, what he thought of them. . . . You can't go on living like this!"

Is this the religion of Jesus Christ—a life that is tense, anxious, gives the impression that Christianity is a heavy burden of things to be done and accounts to be rendered? It was indeed necessary to arouse concern among Christians, force them out of an egoistic tranquillity, and make them discover the challenge of commitment. It was necessary to shake a happiness that was small, virtuous, and facile, that was, in short, insensitive to true charity. For many, however, a certain revision of the hierarchy of values is perhaps necessary today, a certain purification of worldly preoccupations with achievement. We must rise above our cares in a greater serenity and trust in God. Our young people condemn us justly when they denounce our lack of joy.

We must develop an education of joy and optimism. Adolescents will follow with their whole being wherever they find the joy of God. Let the religious communities or apostolic movements that complain of the lack of vocations examine the quality of their joy and hope! Vocations are generally numerous in groups that radiate detachment and evangelical hope, true joy of life. We do not mean a joy which cuts itself off from human reality, but the joy that is born from the sureness of the Lord's presence and of His

victory. We also know how well education generally succeeds in families where there is affection, laughter and joy.

We have said: *to be an event.* The event which young
people seek and which they await is always the same: the
Easter-Event. It is not enough for them to read in the
Gospel that Jesus Christ came out of the tomb one day,
2000 years ago. They must witness, here and now, a beginning of the resurrection of the flesh, in the paths of grace
and hope.

Some will perhaps be surprised at our insistence, throughout these pages, on specifying the kind of presence and relationship that should exist between educators and their students. In our opinion this is the heart of education—today
more than ever—because of the mentality which we have
studied.

We have said that the education of youth is "atmospheric." It depends less on external constraints and ready-
made formulae than on the intense radiation of the charity
of the Church. It is education first of all through identification, through osmosis. In order that they may feel called by
name, young people must sense themselves touched by
Jesus Christ. Jesus Christ today is ourselves, and our faithful
attentiveness to them, despite our profound inadequacy.
Even when we cannot do anything, it is never a waste of
time to listen to them, look at them, love them, with that
joyful hope which the Lord Jesus gives us.

PART THREE

PEDAGOGICAL AND PASTORAL
REFLECTIONS

This third part could more accurately be entitled, "Guidelines for an education of faith of today's youth."

We are not concerned here with a synthesis of the orientations necessary for such an education. We shall simply try to shed some light on the key questions that face educators in actual practice today. We shall also point out certain important accents in the Christian formation of youth. We shall not attempt to say all that could be said, but only to outline certain paths, in the light of current problems.

Perhaps the chief value of these considerations is that they have slowly ripened over the years through teamwork among educators.

CHAPTER SIX

PROBLEMS OF ADOLESCENTS AND
BASIC ORIENTATIONS OF A CHRISTIAN EDUCATION

Every epoch is characterized by certain points or lines of
sensitivity. With the astronomical discoveries of the six-
teenth century, for instance, man had to rethink his place
in the universe and free himself from certain concepts
which he had hitherto linked with his faith. We need only
recall Galileo; or the efforts and Summae of St. Thomas to
integrate into Christianity the ancient philosophic tradi-
tions that were breaking in upon the men of the Middle
Ages.

These key points reveal the limitations of man's conquest
of reality. By the same token, however, they also represent
high points of man's will and spirit, and provide the terrain
for research and struggles, for failures and deviations. In a
Christian context we may speak here of sanctity and fall, of
discovery and heresy.[1]

In studying the adolescents' life of faith, especially in
today's generation, we have noticed certain critical points

---

[1] It has been said that heresies are nothing but distorted truths or
distortions of the truth seeking to define itself. Clarification of doctrine and heresies generally go together.

and lines of sensitivity that are pregnant with dangers as well as with promise. How can we explain their appearance? What are they like? Are they not due to the fact that to-day's youth faces a totally new situation in confronting the world?

Primitive man was dependent on the world. It was a strange, powerful reality that dictated its laws to him. The world was an object of both fear and contemplation, for in its features man discovered quite spontaneously the mark of that creative, all-powerful God on whom nature made him dependent day by day.

With the progressive development of the human spirit, of culture, and power, man became keenly aware of his individuality and personality, and this, especially since the time of the Renaissance. He realized that he was distinct from the world and from other men, and affirmed himself as unique, "original," even autonomous.[2]

In our time, while a certain cult of subjectivity still persists,[3] we witness the appearance of a new relationship between man and the world. It is no longer merely a question of static contemplation or dependence on nature, nor of his individual uniqueness. Man has a new awareness of his dominion over nature and a collective will to confront and

[2] Cf. Romano Guardini, Welt und Person. Also, The End of the Modern World (New York: Sheed and Ward, 1956).

[3] Is this a last flare-up of a trend that is on its way out? It is well known that, in the realm of psychology, the characteristics of a given age flare up again before disappearing, e.g., the transition from child-hood to adolescence, from adulthood to old age. Perhaps this hyper-subjectivity (such as it is revealed in the novels of Sagan, for instance) is the peak of that vague and excessive individualism due to man's new feeling of power over nature.

subdue it. A boy of 15 does not, of course, express himself in such abstract generalities; but he is in actual fact part of a world that views reality in this manner. When he reads *Scientific American* or *Popular Science Monthly* he has the feeling that he will be the agent of progress and benefit from a power and happiness hitherto unknown to man. And when he constructs a radio through his technical skill and the work of his own hands, he is respected by his peers as a worth-while person.

What constitutes both the drama and the wealth of today's youth is their new position in relation to nature and the world of men. This new situation calls forth and develops in them a creative drive in their confrontation with nature, a feeling of power and domination, a keen sensitivity to earthly values.

The educator must be present in these sensitive points "where the Spirit breathes." One of his noblest tasks is to direct young people into those privileged places where they help "make" themselves by bringing their own contribution to history. This task deserves to be undertaken with enthusiasm, but it is also laborious and delicate. The psychological evolution of today's youth has taken a decisive turn which separates it radically from older generations and will set it in a new direction for years to come.

The few orientations we propose here should not be taken as absolute principles. These pages pretend to be neither a theoretical treatise nor an exhaustive treatment of the subject. We would, rather, offer some positive suggestions for a more effective religious education of adolescents.

Man's new relationship to nature poses three great questions and provokes three spontaneous attitudes among young people. While these are often unconscious, they are crucial and permanent and underlie all their other attitudes, from love of popular songs and sports to dreams of human development and progress.

In the first place, young people have a great sense of freedom, especially in creating their own values. Man becomes drunk with his conquests and confused belief that tomorrow the world will in very deed be the prolongation of his being, his "mystical body," according to the expression of Urs von Balthasar. Hence his keen sense of creative work, action and achievement.

Secondly, they have a great awareness of social, universal, and cosmic realities. Among the best of them especially, the sense of social responsibility has now awakened, the taste for vast syntheses, and the idea of a history en route toward perfection and unity.

Finally, they are sensitive to human realities and temporal values. Because they live in a world profoundly at grips with nature and intoxicated with its discoveries, they know the price and taste the value of contact with the earth and the world of men. This makes them hypersensitive to things, life, human values, and temporal commitments.

These three aspirations, arising primarily from the needs of our time, find an echo in their psychology and parallel the stages of maturing in adolescence.

At the stage of pubescent adolescence, it is the last of the three quests—sensitivity to human values—which plays the greatest role, because it corresponds to the great passions of this age. From the boy who spends all his time with his radio or TV and is fascinated by billboards and comic strips, to the young college student who goes from exam to exam, from movie to coke joint—each of these young people is plunged into a vast world of knowledge and violent sensations.

It is not only pubescent adolescence which arouses the appetites, but also the age in which we live. "I personally don't care much whether I am unhappy or not," says Françoise Sagan. "It doesn't matter! What matters is to live, to have desires, ambitions, dreams, to be propelled by a sort of power." Passion! This is the great profession of faith of many young people. And how many timid, impoverished Christians look with envy at the independent, fiery vitality of their non-Christian brothers!

With the advent of maturity the affective exuberance of puberty will gradually subside and become more moderate. As he approaches young adulthood, the age of socialization, and of entering the occupational world, the adolescent awakens from his subjective fancies and becomes aware of the values of creative freedom, human work, temporal commitment, and social success. The thirst for life now becomes the desire for action and for recognition by his fellows.

He now leaves behind the quests of puberty. To his desire for friendship and joy of living, love of sports and self-development, is added the thirst to create. He feels the need to have a function, to accomplish a worth-while work on earth and to be appreciated by other men.

In addition to the development of his subjective processes we now notice the growth of his social awareness and will to create.

But there are dangers inherent in the adolescents' quest. And the educator often feels helpless in the face of all this turmoil. He is afraid of being unfaithful to the Gospel, which calls the poor blessed and closes the Kingdom to those who possess the earth. His fear is not illusory. Any answer we give, any proclamation of the Good News must have measured not only the rich possibilities of this world but also its risks, ambiguities, and weak points.

In suggesting the direction of a possible solution we must be aware of the dangers. We shall point out three in particular and thereby suggest three main positive orientations.

The first is self-sufficiency; this is by far the greatest danger of all. The Pharisees of old settled down complacently in the Law. Today's Pharisees are in danger of feeling complacent in their conquests. They cling jealously to their creative action or physical vitality, as though these were their own. How easy it is to become intoxicated with academic degrees, worldly success, social prestige! How easily we climb the slope of a human glory acquired through the precision of machines, exactness of mathematics, and achievements of technology!

One type of self-sufficiency comes from the pride of domination. There is another kind, no less harmful, which comes from the pride of being one's own world. We surround ourselves with material goods. Even though they constitute a powerful incentive to human activity, they are at the same time terrible snares. The power of the flesh is the mightiest of all torrents—not, as we might think at first, because it carries away and ravages man, but because it throws him back upon himself. The greatest danger of the use of material goods is not stultification, but deification and idolatry.

Our whole education should, therefore, aim at communicating a sense of dependence, of spiritual poverty and spiritual childhood. This orientation is basic. It should not be the prerogative of an elite but should be preached to all. It is surely not in vain that St. Thérèse of the Child Jesus is acclaimed as the saint of our time.

Then there are the natural deviations. St. Augustine's words are more applicable today than ever: "The passions dragged me by the garments of my flesh." How can you avoid being swept away by feelings and subjective needs when you are 15 or 20 and live in the 1960s? A cold education of the will is not enough.[4] The young person's affective powers must be channelled and given a positive orientation.

Would an education to a set of ideals suffice? In by-gone days education strongly insisted on ideals, the pursuit of a goal, fidelity to principles. To the masters of the Christian life this meant the Christianizing of youth's drive toward a goal outside itself. We need only recall the trend, since the Renaissance, toward a growing awareness of the individual's worth. Despite the risks of idealism this was a valid orientation, since it aimed to integrate the wealth of the epoch as well as that of the adolescent's instincts.

Today, however, young people are less easily attracted by an ideal outside themselves, and much more by concrete

[4] E.g., phrases like "Get your will under control," which are more pagan than Christian.

tasks, human relationships, and practical achievements. It is not so much a question of my relationship to "the ideal Me" as of my relation to the world. In this context it has become necessary, without excluding the education to idealism, to emphasize another direction.

In our educational system the idea of vocation or mission should replace the idea of "aiming for the stars"; not "my ideal," but "awareness of the other" and fidelity to the Holy Spirit at work in history.[5]

Since young people are so sensitive to human, earthly realities, and since they will soon be at grips with nature in order to dominate and utilize it through technology, let us teach them to look at these realities with the eyes of faith. Let them discover the possibility of a holy love of this earth. Let us teach them to act and create in the name of God, that is, "by vocation."

We must educate young people to an awareness, in faith and charity, of human, earthly realities[6]—to an education of freedom in the consciousness of their God-given vocation and mission.

The third danger is anxiety. Karl Rahner points out that Catholicism today is in danger of losing the values of individuality. The personality is in danger of being dissolved in anonymity. Though the adolescent seems less susceptible to this danger because he remains psychologically highly indi-

---

[5] It is only a question of emphasis. It would be a mistake to oppose the two orientations, or to condemn one in favor of the other.

[6] Cf. the approach of Catholic Action, which responds to a specific need of the times.

vidual, even individualistic—at least when he has the time and possibility to be himself and has access to a certain cultural level. It is true, nevertheless, that the sudden appearance of modern industrial and technological achievements and means of leisure and escape, as well as the crushing weight of sociological limitations (particularly among minority groups), seriously threaten to sweep the young person into inconsistency of character and dreams of easy success.

In the case of highly emotional young people the educator should try to help them overcome their anxiety and fears. Among the disillusioned and so-called realistic ones, on the other hand, he must work against lack of commitment and desire for evasion. In this respect we should stress personal participation in the life of the community, and emphasize the sense of vocation, of unique mission in the Church and world that is lovingly entrusted to us by the Lord of Life.

To educate the "spirit of childhood" and of alert charity within a living Christian comunity, and to awaken each one's personal mission in this world, should be the main accents in our education of today's youth. Are we not, here, at the very heart of the Gospel?

We shall elaborate on these main points in the chapters that follow. In the context of catechesis we shall show that the true meaning of life is charity animated by the spirit of Easter and Pentecost. Next, we shall consider these points in the light of pedagogical orientations. The perspectives we shall outline may seem demanding. Some will perhaps consider them beyond the ability of many young people. What, then, of the Gospel and of St. Paul?

If the formulation appears complex and the explanations seem difficult, teachers will know how to adapt them—not, however, by watering down the demands of the Kingdom, but by penetrating to that central point where all is simple because all is profound.

CHAPTER SEVEN

MAIN LINES OF CATECHESIS

During adolescence the educator will try to shed light on the road that lies ahead and to prepare his students effectively for a mature Christian life. The Christian message must be re-presented at this time, but in a new perspective, with different accents from the catechesis given in childhood. The emphasis of our teaching will correspond to the sensitive points mentioned earlier, which make operative the great mysteries of salvation, Easter and Pentecost.

During puberty, the teacher should shed light on the meaning of life and human values. Hence a catechesis is called for that will reveal the full meaning and consequences for man's destiny of the redemptive Incarnation. It is Easter that sheds light on the meaning of life and death, the meaning of joy, effort, and human success, and on the meaning of the realities of this world. Because it is the climax of the drama of death and life, the Paschal Mystery will be the ultimate point of reference of our teaching. In its light we can explain to the adolescent the true meaning of his questions and supply an answer to what he seeks.

Toward the end of adolescence and at the time of young adulthood, we must evangelize the creative drive which propels the young person toward the earth and the world of men. There is need at this time for a continuous catechesis of vocation and mission which the Lord entrusts to man, in the light of Pentecost. What will this catechesis of the Mystery of Easter or of Pentecost be like?

It is not a question of an academic course on Easter, or of presenting Easter all by itself—however beautiful and apologetically valuable such a course might be. Rather, we must reveal the consequences of the Paschal Mystery for the adolescents' lives by showing how the destiny of the earth and the universe flows from this intervention of God in the world. Only through concrete application will they really understand, here and now, the meaning of the Resurrection or of the sending of the Holy Spirit. In working with young people it is essential that we make the link between the Paschal Mystery and their lives.

The redemptive Incarnation and its full unfolding— Christmas, Easter, Pentecost—is not one event among others, some sort of doctrinal or historical event. It is THE event, in whose light we must illuminate the whole of Christian doctrine and moral teaching in a living, concrete manner. It should become our constant Leitmotiv or rather, the living axis of our entire catechical synthesis. This is true at all times but especially today, because of the concrete, historical mentality of young people.

A Catechesis of Life

Young people are by nature sensitive to the values of the world. They believe in progress because "the future is theirs." They love Rock 'n Roll because it intoxicates or relaxes them. They love life because they are bursting with vitality and the world seems rich in promise. This is the morality which so many movie stars preach to them.[1]

To all these young Christians who seek only worldly success the Church does not cease to say with Jesus: "Do not the pagans do as much?" Or, "Little children, guard yourselves from idols" (1 John 5:21).

We need a Christian education in human realities. Shall we teach flight from the world? Or love of the world? Never before, perhaps, was there as great a need to proclaim the true meaning of life and love of the world as in this age of frenzied love for life.

Woe to those who preach only a *black Christianity*, symbolized by death and flight from the world! They are unfaithful to the Resurrection of Jesus and to the hope of youth. Besides, no one will listen to them!

On the other hand, it is equally mistaken to preach a Christianity of a purely natural joy of life, as though religion were nothing more than a stepping stone to limitless life and the desire for conquest. These in turn are unfaithful to eternal life and to hope in the joy of God, this joy which no man can take from us and which the Holy Spirit inspires deep in young people's hearts.

It is in the light of the Paschal Mystery, fully understood and lived, that young people will perceive the true meaning

[1] We are reminded here of the emotion stirred up among many young people (especially girls) by the death of Marilyn Monroe in 1962. Having identified themselves with the movie star's exuberance of life they suddenly lapse, with her death, into fruitless brooding. But they forget quickly, there are other stars . . .

of their life, of their drive toward the future, and their hunger for success and conquest.

The meaning of a life united to Christ's Pasch is to offer oneself totally to the Lord of Life in order to grow, die, and rise in glory to a fullness of communion, rich in all the humanity acquired during one's earthly sojourn. In a style that is simple, close to Revelation and the humble facts of daily life, we should introduce adolescents to this fundamental theme of Claudel's works:

"The purpose of life is not to live. The feet of the children of God are not bound to this wretched earth. It is not a question of living, but of dying. Not a question of building a cross, but mounting it and giving what we have joyfully. That is what is meant by joy and freedom, by grace and eternal youth."[2]

Such is the meaning of our earthly sojourn and of the dynamism of human life. The goal of man's life is not to lead us to the jealously autonomous possession of ourselves, but to bring us ultimately to a self-giving that is ever more consistent, free, and fully human. It is this that the Paschal Mystery reveals, when God exalts His Son from the very depth of His abandonment.

We must preach such a meaning of life "in season and out of season," since the zest for life has no other meaning than this.[3]

[2] The Tidings Brought to Mary, Act IV, Scene 2.
[3] We must not oppose cross and happiness. Understanding the language of the cross always remains the criterion of Christian sanctity, but only if we understand it rightly. The cross is not an end, nor an absolute apart from the idea of happiness and vital growth. The cross is within the context of the Resurrection. The cross is for

Our catechesis, then, should be one that imparts love for earthly realities. And this, even though we know that many, confronted with these perspectives, will exclaim: "Of what use, then, is the world? Of what use are our instincts and body?"

Even while we proclaim the meaning of life, it is very important that we discern the Christian meaning of the world and of tangible mediations. Man's confrontation with the world, the drive of his instincts and the power of material reality—all this is meant to give great force to our human effort. All this is ours, not for the sake of selfish possession but for a more perfect, free, and rich self-giving to the Lord of Life and Glory.[4]

---

the sake of the Resurrection. That is to say, the understanding of suffering is in the context of understanding man's desire for happiness. The more a person chooses happiness, for the sake of full vital growth, the more he chooses the cross, the more firmly he grasps the cross in happiness and happiness in the cross.

No doubt it will take young people a long time to discover such implications. God teaches us Redemption only in the Covenant, that is, slowly, progressively. Although the catechist must not water down the quality of the life promised by God, he must wisely measure the "doses" in which he proclaims the Message. Jesus said to Peter: "When thou wast young thou didst gird thyself and walk where thou wouldst. But when thou art old thou wilt stretch forth thy hands, and another will gird thee, and lead thee where thou wouldst not" (John 21:18).

[4] In speaking to young people of the mystery of the Eucharist and its meaning in relation to the whole universe, we can show the triple meaning of the confrontation of human and earthly realities: 1) giving intensity to the offering. Whether it is a matter of work or of rest, man "makes" himself in his encounter with other men and in his confrontation with earthly realities. He perfects himself both as individual and as community. Will this not bring added wealth to his eucharistic offering? 2) providing "matter for consecration." Man's offering in Christ is destined for consecration. The earth

200   PEDAGOGICAL REFLECTIONS

Are we faithful to God's plan if we ignore or despise the instincts and powerful energy which throb in young people's hearts, especially in their relationship to earthly goods and mediations? Let us instead evangelize this drive which carries them toward the earth and man, so that in fostering human growth it will not become a selfish grasp of things, but a more total, generous gift of self.

We should not oppose their love of sports and life, the enthusiasm with which they pursue a human task, their need for leisure; for if we do we shall be opposing God, who has willed that our spiritual drives be supported and stimulated by temporal, physical realities.

From a friend's handshake to the grandiose vista of a mountain range, all earthly realities bear within them the possibility of giving depth and intensity to our impulse toward charity. It is in this sense that we must constantly illuminate them, giving them transparency and shape.

How is such an education to be achieved? In our cate-

---

which man stamps with his presence, and man himself, raised by his work and his rest, are gradually taken up by God in Christ. Until "God is all in all" the eucharistic host is the sign that the realities of the future have already begun. 3) realizing progressively the communion of persons and the unity of the world in the Body of Christ. Men are called to unite through earthly mediations, gestures of love, etc., as well as through their confrontation with the earth. It is in the eucharistic communion that human unity is divinely fashioned and finds its point of highest intensity. It is also from this point that man, "communed, eucharistized," is sent back into the world for the sake of a new offering and consecration. We are often surprised that young people are bored by our teaching on the Eucharist. If we were capable of showing them its meaning in relation to their life and to all of human and earthly reality, they would yawn less frequently!

chesis it is important to understand clearly that the whole of material reality constitutes for man both a stimulant and a terrible risk of imprisonment and deviation. It is by being faithful to the spirit of Easter that young people will be able to live in this world and make the right use of material realities. This requires a threefold attitude on their part, which we must present in the proper balance: First, their attitude should be one of faith and positive love. They may not despise this earth from which God has made His Body in Christ. They must learn to see and love it as Christ sees and loves it in His redemptive Incarnation. The catechist must foster this positive, supernatural outlook.

Secondly, they should understand asceticism and death positively. Sustained by the life of the Church they must take up their Cross and do penance, in order that the limits of the world might be stretched and the deviations destroyed or repaired.[5] Even if they do not yet have a true understanding of death and suffering, we may not avoid the issue under pretext of adapting to the world's view. If we do, our teaching will be false. We must, however, teach the cross in relation to the joyous and glorious aspect of Easter.

Thirdly, they should be filled with the spirit of offering and service. For, they are to offer to God and their brothers, in an impulse of profound charity, all the energy which they have discovered in the use of material reality, all the growth in value they have gained in confronting and "assuming" the earth. Thus the catechist will show them that it is little by little, through the work of their entire lives, that the uni-

[5] We can surmount the dangers only by accepting the Lord's mercy: the sacrament of penance, etc.

verse is brought back to the Father in a personal response, like a "great offering of praise."

To sum up: we shall illuminate and educate their use of material mediations so that, far from constituting an earthly paradise, the latter will instead serve the renewal of charity and guarantee a mutual enrichment on both the personal and collective levels.

Our catechesis must thus be linked to the total human reality. And such an education should not be left to chance. It must permeate our catechesis of Christ, of morality, of the Church. Our catechesis will be incomplete as long as a single earthly reality is excluded from the vision of faith.

Thus, in speaking of friendship it is not enough to discuss psychological laws and lay down rules of conduct. We must also show how Christ takes to Himself man's natural affinities (Incarnation);[6] requires the renunciation of all that pertains to the "old man" (death); achieves a fullness of communion among men (Resurrection); this fullness begins here on earth, but will reach completion only in the communion in glory (Parousia).

We shall constantly refer all subjective impulses and human realities to the standard of interpretation found in salvation history. These revelatory events (creation, Incarnation, Pentecost and Parousia—all contained and achieved in Easter) will permit us to see each reality in a full, balanced light.

[6] It is important to show that Christ does not destroy but raises up and saves. Christ destroys only sin, and it is precisely sin that limits and destroys life.

The witness of the catechist and of the community is extremely important. At the age of 15 one does not spontaneously confide one's human joys and thirst for life to the Risen Lord. Our catechesis, therefore, must be lively and reassuring, serious and dynamic at the same time, promising a fullness of life.[7]

In unfolding the Paschal Mystery we must vigorously proclaim, through the necessary dying, "the hope of our calling by God, the riches of the glory of His inheritance in the saints, and the exceeding greatness of His power toward us who believe. Its measure is the working of His mighty power, which He has wrought in Christ in raising Him from the dead" (Eph. 1:19–21).

Such a Paschal catechesis will carry all the more weight if it is actually lived by the catechist and the Christian community. In order to proclaim the Easter of all things in the Lord words alone are not enough, especially for adolescents. They must be complemented by a living witness and experience.

When young people have learned that Jesus came not to destroy but to bring life in its fullness—that He came, not to quench the joy of life but to give "that joy which no one shall take from you," then they will be better prepared for the struggles of this century. They will be better equipped for both love and renunciation.

In the vision of faith which the Paschal Mystery gives

[7] We stress this aspect of sure, serious, and realistic affirmation that catechesis of adolescents should have. Together with St. John we should say to those who are unsure about the direction of their lives: "These words are certain and true."

them, they will realize that it is good to live, work, and achieve a great task. They will accomplish this not for selfish ends, but so that the world of men may become a little more the world of God in charity, until one day everything —they themselves and this earth which bears their imprint —may be invaded by the Glory of God "through the power which raised Jesus Christ from the dead."

It is not enough to give them the taste of true life in relation to Christ's redemptive act. We must also open up and guarantee the meaning of that life in relation to the eschatological dimensions of Christ's Pasch. Only if we constantly keep the goal in view will the things we encounter on the way retain their true meaning.

It is in the light of the Last Things, proclaimed in word and deed, that human realities will keep a transcendent quality and permanent tension toward the "above" of the Resurrection. "Seek the things that are above, savor the things of heaven."

In their commitment to the things of this earth young people will need to be shown again the transcendent meaning of history. In their daily distraction amid the dazzle of things, they need to hear the proclamation of their homeland, "where true joys are to be found."[8]

It is normal that in our times when history plays such an important role, biblical eschatology should regain its rightful place in catechesis. A certain Platonic, idealized, and dis-

---

[8] In *The Centurion's Journey* Psychari takes up the theme of the Fourth Sunday after Easter: ". . . that amidst all the vicissitudes of this life, our hearts may be fixed where true joys are to be found."

embodied way of talking about heaven makes the young generation yawn or shiver. Experience shows that it is quite otherwise with a presentation of eschatological realities that is biblical, personal, and concrete. This is the kind of presentation they await, which our faith obliges us to proclaim.[9]

How is this to be done? By word and deed, we have said. Let us be more specific; first of all, "by word."

The eschatological realities must be proclaimed at all times, with vigor and earnestness, as the ultimate dimension of all that exists.

It will often be advisable to begin our catechesis of adolescents with a proclamation of the Last Things: glory before grace, the eternal reality of love before its earthly realizations, etc. For it is the destination rather than the roads to it that will arouse their attention and awaken their desire. Thus, we should speak to this generation in terms of happiness, value, and paradise, before we speak in terms of knowledge, the conditions for admission, or the ways that lead to the goal.

At the same time the categories of thought and the analogies we use are particularly important here. What has frequently disgusted too many young people with the great final realities of existence is a falsely idealistic or theatrical presentation. We must be honest. Let us not try primarily to move, but to reveal. Let us take for our catechesis the categories of thought closest to their daily experience, cate-

[9] Cf. Congar, The Wide World, My Parish. We know from experience that young people want us to tell them about the "great truths," including hell.

gories and analogies of interpersonal relationships: the banquet, marriage, leaving the family, etc. . . . These are, moreover, the very categories of the Bible.

And then, "by deed." We shall speak in vain of the Kingdom of the Resurrection if young people do not have before their eyes the living witness of the Church—simultaneously committed and detached—in the lives of Christians, priests, and religious. Such a catechesis "by deed" can alone compensate for that other, perverted "catechesis" achieved every day by advertising, the movies, and worldly values.

The life of religious presents a special problem for today's adolescent. We must answer it carefully, for it pinpoints the world's incomprehension of the Kingdom of God. What teacher has not sooner or later come up against the objection: "What use are these monks and nuns, since they don't do anything for this world? We don't need these useless people!" In the light of what we have said of the contemporary mentality, such a question will not come as a surprise to us. Yet we would be to blame if our proclamation of the Gospel did not sooner or later awaken in the hearts of young people an awareness of the greatness of the religious life and the taste for the heavenly life. How are we to do this?

In the first place we must know how to proclaim with conviction the splendors of grace and glory that are in store for us. Baptism, which has introduced us into the Mystical Body of the Risen Christ, makes of us radically new creatures. We are dead to sin and belong entirely to God. We are creatures "whose conversation is in heaven." Let us clearly point out the immense value of this new human

condition inaugurated in Christ. We must be able to re-
capture the concrete, vigorous style of the Apostles and
Fathers of the Church.[10] Like Jesus to the Samaritan
woman, we must unveil the secrets of the Kingdom, the
marvels of the living water, until eternal life becomes the
thing most desired, until the state of mankind risen to the
life of the Kingdom becomes more precious than the transitory life of earth.

Next, we must transform the adolescent's desire for human fullness. We must be able to show that, in the perspective of Easter, the act of total giving which does not shrink
back even from death is more "living" than the act of acquiring and dominating. The offering of our humanity is
more perfect than the acquisition of that humanity.[11] Heavenly life is the goal of earthly life, the building's completion
is the goal of its construction. Strange though these realities
may appear to adolescents whose eyes are riveted to the
earth, we must affirm them lest we degrade the Kingdom.

In doing this we shall not deprecate the vocation of man,
which is to "make" himself by means of this earth, and to
make this earth for God. We shall, however, affirm that the
ultimate act of offering and giving is more perfect than the
act of conquest, that the Kingdom of God is greater than
this earth.

Ultimately, of course, one's life decision depends on each

[10] We might read St. Peter's First Epistle, or the Letter to the
Ephesians, in this light. It is a matter of "trembling with unspeak-
able joy, full of glory" at the thought of the full revelation of Christ
and His Salvation.

[11] It is important to help our students understand the Christian
meaning of death, as summit of life.

one's personal vocation in the Kingdom. This must be stressed emphatically.

To the *religious* is given by special vocation the grace to realize his own fulfillment with a minimum of earthly mediations and material goods. He has also received through his vocation the grace to live in a more radical attitude of offering and self-giving, in anticipation of the heavenly life. Is not this a state of fullness and perfection?

The *Christian lay person*, also, by vocation acquires, possesses, "assumes," and offers. Thus his commitment prepares a fullness of the earth's great Yes to God. This is, in its own way, a reality of extraordinary supernatural grace— vocation in the full sense of the word.

Man's vocation, whatever its nature, is full human development, joy of living, and creative urge, because it comes from the God of Love—if only we are able to see it with the eyes of faith.

The adolescent is exceedingly sensitive to the question of vocation and of the different "ages of man." We should speak to him of this at length. We should show that providentially, in every man's life, the age of youth is especially oriented toward acquiring, the age of adulthood toward giving, old age toward that climax of giving which is abandonment of self and all that one has acquired and created. . . . The first stage should culminate in the last.[12]

---

[12] We should not hesitate to describe fully to adolescents the stages of life and their Christian meaning. This will help them realize concretely the implications of Easter for themselves and their future—(For a description of the "ages of man" see Guardini, *Les âges de la vie.*—Trans.)

Religious life should be presented in its relation to the Christianization of temporal realities. Many adolescents ask one question about religious life: How can they, with their thirst for life, expect to become religious, or even appreciate religious life, if the latter appears to be devoid of earthly, human values?[13]

Here it is important to make them think about the following points: First, one enters religious life through a vocation to the fullness of life. This fullness already possesses by anticipation nuances of the absolute and infinite that do not exist on the level of purely human limitations. This fullness is poverty of spirit and joy of offering, liberation from the ambiguities of the flesh and from temporal involvements for the sake of contemplation, the essential act of love, and for a more total service of our brothers in this world.[14]

Secondly, the intensity, the palpable urge of the earthly realities left behind is more than compensated for by a world of grace which cannot be called into question, and which already rewards a hundredfold in this world the man who is faithful.

Finally, religious have a unique role to play in the earthly community, in Christianizing earthly realities. We believe that adolescents are very sensitive to this motive for a reli-

[13] Young people have often mentioned this difficulty to us. Cf. the study in *Lumen Vitae*, VIII, No. 4 (1953), pp. 639 ff.

[14] Traditionally the religious remains in the service of his brothers in the world, especially in all that is most humble, in the works of mercy, etc.; and he announces the Gospel among the poor. Cf. Congar, *Vie Spirituelle* (September, 1959).

gious vocation, because they so readily think in terms of "mission."

Let us not be afraid to develop this last aspect. The Christian needs the religious and their eschatological witness, much as the Frenchman in the occupied zone during World War II needed contact with the Underground, in order to keep alive his sense of freedom.[15]

The Christian will appreciate temporal values more readily if they are fully authentic, if they keep their "salt," that is, the attraction and urge of the realities of the Resurrection. These do not, indeed, lessen or destroy human values, but on the contrary consecrate them and bring them to their full realization.

The catechist must clearly define here the eschatological significance of religious life in the world and for the world. Religious are a reminder of the days of fullness to come, and they inspire other Christians to a sense of excellence, perfection, and total giving. Far from being useless to their times, they snatch us from the dangers of pagan ensnarement in order to cast us, and the entire earth, into the arms of God. They are the guarantee that the world as we know it is transitory, that its limitations and ambiguities will pass away. They say to the rest of men until the end of time: "When you shall see all these things come to pass lift up your heads, for your deliverance is at hand . . . Watch and pray, that this day will not find you weighted down in rioting and drunkenness."

They proclaim the world of freedom and love, of service

[15] Congar, ibid.

and mercy in all its fullness.[16] They proclaim, finally, that the resurrection of the flesh is possible and true.

If educators know how to speak concretely through both word and deed,[17] if young people live in a community of the Church which is *in* the world but not *of* the world, they will, in accepting grace, open their souls to an earthly life that is evangelical, and which retains the savor of "the things that are above," as the Mass of Easter promises.

Catechesis of Freedom and of Vocation

According to the studies we have been able to make the catechetical theme which arouses the greatest interest at every age is that of vocation; and that which arouses the greatest number of questions is undoubtedly freedom.

Young people feel the need to go beyond the negative criticisms which the natural sciences make and which stifle

[16] It is necessary to elaborate on this point here because of the frequent criticisms made by young people of religious engaged in teaching. When we say that religious proclaim the eschatological character of earthly realities we are not saying that they proclaim a "disembodied and disincarnate kingdom." In the case of a nun, for instance, it is not a question of loving young people with a pseudo-angelic, "metaphysical" love. This does not proclaim the Kingdom but ideas! The love of religious should have a certain delicacy, humble attentiveness, and also warmth, which give a foretaste of the spiritual plenitude of the Kingdom. It must also have that essentially heavenly quality which is both highly personal, unique, and universal.

[17] A young woman told a priest: "Father, we want you to be both very close to us and very pure, so that we can believe that the Kingdom is possible and true!" A visit to a monastery can be one of the best forms of catechesis.

their thirst for the infinite. At the same time, accustomed as they are through the positive sciences to analysis and mathematical precision, they want to be able to base their faith on solid, objective realities. In confronting the world which offers itself to their youthful vitality, they wonder about God's view of it: Is He for? Is He against?

Neither apologetics nor practical action will suffice to illuminate and give shape to such quests. The young person's intellect seeks illumination in the solid knowledge of a God who intervenes objectively in his destiny. His will aspires to commit itself to life, not only through instinctual drives, but through a mission entrusted to him by God.

This situation requires of the educator a serious catechesis of freedom and vocation.

"When I joined the army," wrote a young Catholic who had grown up in a sheltered atmosphere, "my fellow recruits told me: 'You smell of incense.'" And the same boy concluded: "We Catholics have no guts!"

Millions of young people suffer from a sort of Christian inferiority complex. They feel imprisoned by prejudices, guilt, by inhibitions which handicap them greatly, both in their relationships and in facing the realites of life.

In contrast to their comrades' self-assurance and dynamism they feel like weak, sickly children, overwhelmed by life and oppressed by the law.[18] Some of them think that in order to be free they must escape from the Church and throw off the burden of religious principles.

[18] This reproach comes more particularly from students who are too much pent up in certain religious institutions or groups.

Is this not another way, in today's concrete and living situation, of accusing God and the Church of alienation? Because they are in a world that is undergoing a severe crisis of autonomy and the rejection of all authority, these young people are exposed to a similar crisis.[19]

How can we give a positive orientation to our catechesis of freedom?

In working with early adolescence it is important to follow a concrete, biblical approach rather than a philosophical one, to which the young people are not yet particularly open. Our catechesis of freedom will therefore start, not from vague discussions on the existence of free will which generally lead nowhere, but from whatever positive experience of true freedom they may have had. We shall help them discover that their happiest times were perhaps when they arranged something to their own liking and taste (maybe their rooms); when they organized a Sunday trip; when they formed a team of two or more to do some fascinating job. We shall also show them that they feel free each time they love someone.

Thus we shall from the beginning link freedom and creation, freedom and love in their minds. Whatever the nature of our catechesis, we must never lose sight of these cate-

[19] At the beginning of adolescence the desire for freedom reveals the need for breaking out of the external protections of childhood in which one feels imprisoned. Between 18 and 25 the problem appears under a different guise, and reveals ultimately the need to escape—not from external restrictions, but from oneself. It has now become a need for liberation rather than a need for freedom to do whatever one wants. It seems to us that the problem is particularly serious at this time, and that the faith itself is now at stake, in its interior logic.

gories. We must steer clear of a freedom defined solely in terms of free will, a fortiori in terms of freedom to do as one pleases. We must show with reference to a living experience that this latter is in reality only loneliness and disillusionment.

After we have made the distinction between free will and freedom and have linked freedom and value, we must develop a biblical catechesis and show the Christian meaning of true freedom.[20]

We should show that Christian freedom is participation in the creative and saving action of God. We should show, through the Bible and through subjective experience, that supreme freedom consists in sharing, by faith and charity, in the infinite vitality of God. From Genesis to the Apocalypse, the whole of the Bible reveals that "freedom is the condition of those who belong wholly to God"[21] and who live as His own.

For older adolescents, for those who are open to modern currents of thought and a more intellectual approach, it is important to base these facts on rational reflection. In this way we shall demystify[22] the idea of alienation that slumbers in the depths of their imagination, and which Marxism can keep alive.[23]

[20] Cf. A. Brien in Verité et Vie (October, 1958).—Also J. Mouroux, The Meaning of Man (New York: Sheed and Ward, n.d.).

[21] Jean-Jacques von Allmen, Vocabulaire biblique, p. 157.

[22] Demystify: clarifying a truth by bringing out the lie which is hidden beneath the words.

[23] All sorts of expressions current among people in general express this idea: "I didn't ask to be born," "God is always right," "What does he care anyway?" etc.

Here we must show above all that, ontologically, God is not outside of, but interior to, us. To be free is to recognize God as our source—not a source outside of us and foreign to us but more interior to us than we are to ourselves: *intimidor intimo meo*. Far from being opposed to man's autonomy, God is its very source. To make oneself, to be free and to do what one wants in the full sense of the term, is to recognize and love this Source, which is our most intimate being.

We must make this very clear to adolescents.

Man refuses instinctively to be led by "another," to be directed from the outside. It is this that constitutes dependence and alienation. In order to live man needs a private sphere where he can be absolutely himself in his actions and relationships. Do belief in God and life in the Church indeed mean passing under the yoke of "another"?[24] If they do, man is right in rejecting them.

"My own self cannot exist by remaining in another's power, even if this other is God. . . ." And what if I love the other? "Even if I am in love, the eternal presence of the other would be unbearable."

The fundamental error of this dialogue among Marx, Sartre, the modern mentality, and Christianity stems from the fact that we falsely clothe God with the mask of "the other." God is neither another in relation to His creation, nor is He identical with it. He is God. He creates man, that is, He is the very source of all autonomy and existence. Whatever is uniquely self in a person is rooted in Him. No

---

[24] Romano Guardini, in *Welt und Person*, has studied this problem at length. We draw largely upon his thought here.

comparison can adequately explain this relation of God to man as source of his existence and freedom. If we use the image of a child born of his mother, we must clearly bring out the difference between the creative act of God and the act of the mother, who is only pro-creator.

To establish the Being of God as necessary for man's existence, for his greatness and development, must be one of our major preoccupations in catechesis at this time of subjective turmoil. Woe to us if we make God appear as a facultative quantity or as a vague response to man's needs! In catechesis generally, and especially in the catechesis of freedom, we must show clearly that God does not permit man to call Him into account.[25]

These realities are difficult to grasp for the adolescent, especially for girls, who are less sensitive to the category of being. With them we should emphasize the catechesis of love and happiness, stressing, however, that God is fundamentally both Being and Love. We should present the necessity for God in the light of the demands of human freedom.

Thus, if we would avoid the three dangers that lie in wait for their faith (anxiety, rebellion, and indifference) we must teach both boys and girls to recognize their divine Source under three aspects: as Being, Tenderness, and Mercy.

Unless, as we have just explained, we teach them to

[25] We have in mind here unconsciously blasphemous phrases such as: "Why did God do this?" "I am no longer free since there is a God who always has the last word," etc. See the analysis of faith above, pp. 23 ff.

recognize God as Source of Being, there will be either indifference or revolt against alienation. God will no longer be for them the One who Is. Thus creation establishes the necessity of God for the existence of human freedom.

Unless we teach them to recognize God as Tenderness, there will be anxiety or revolt against exploitation. They must recognize in faith that God has guaranteed, through His life and death in history, that He neither is nor ever will be someone who exploits man. Thus the redemptive Incarnation establishes the necessity of God for man's happiness, and for the growth of his freedom.

Unless we teach them to recognize God as Mercy, there will be despair, for man is no longer lovable and able to love himself. Thus Redemption establishes the necessity of God for the salvation of human freedom.

Finally, such a catechesis of God and of human freedom must lead to a clear demonstration of the precise meaning of divine jealousy in the light of the quest of youthful subjectivity. Through the Covenant in His blood, God has shown decisively wherein His jealousy consists. The jealousy of God: this biblical expression does not mean that God will take advantage of man or will despotically bind man to Himself. It means that God desires the greatness of man, who is ontologically and necessarily tied to Him by nature, to the point that also by grace he may become a child of God, in a relationship of unprecedented friendship.

When young people have understood the *Gloria Dei vivens homo* of St. Irenaeus ("the glory of God is man fully alive"), then freedom will cease to be a problem for them.

Our catechesis of vocation should not be assigned a place of secondary importance, but should be a constant element in our presentation of the Good News to adolescents. Each word "that comes forth from the mouth of God" must resound like a call in the midst of their desires and boredom. In what way may we speak of the whole of catechesis as a call?

In order to determine the necessary conditions if a word is to become call, let us consider the process of interpersonal relationships involved in a call and discern its consequences for catechesis.

To call someone by name is first of all to recognize his potentialities, that special place where he is "potentially" unique and original. The first act of calling consists in this positive recognition of the other's possibilities.

This means that our proclamation must be such that the adolescent can recognize and discover himself within the very message that we proclaim. Let us take the catechesis of grace as an example. If we speak of grace as of an objective entity, the functioning of which we describe in much the same way as we describe a power plant, the adolescent will not recognize himself; grace will be for him something extrinsic to himself. On the other hand, if we speak of grace as of a personal act, infinitely positive and creative, through which God awakens our lowly need for life and happiness so that we may enter into His fullness of life, then the adolescent cannot fail to see that he is recognized and known by God with love. What God has to say to him will not leave him indifferent.

To call someone by name is, furthermore, to make him

discover his own uniqueness. This implies that our proclamation of the Good News must help the adolescent discover his unique characteristics and his place in history as willed by God.

In this respect it is very important that we make clear to him the spiritual significance of his age, temperament, education and events of his life.[26] Thus each one's individual drive will no longer appear simply as natural instinct, but as a calling. Affinities and antipathies will no longer be merely psychological traits, but indications from God.

Thirdly, to call someone by name is to accompany him positively in his process of growth, and to confirm him in his potentialities. This mean that we must ceaselessly proclaim the God of the Covenant. We must preach, not "the great bachelor of the world," but the God of Jesus Christ who enters into dialogue with man in history, accompanies him throughout his human development so as to reassure, correct, and call him to go beyond himself. In our catechesis we must teach adolescents who ask for signs that God is pedagogically, tangibly, effectively present to them. The God of the Old Testament and of the Incarnation has not disappeared. He continues to follow each of us personally, accompanying us with His Presence and His Salvation all the days of our earthly sojourn.

Because of the realistic and concrete mentality of today's youth we believe that the best catechetical procedure is to

[26] Especially in the catechesis of moral and spiritual life. The art of pleasing, the desire to succeed, individual talents, each one's particular capabilities: everything must be "evangelized," that is, illuminated by Jesus Christ.

refer actual problems and events to the solutions and events of salvation history. Let us take some examples: periods of dryness in the life of prayer to Elias in the desert; the zest for living to the life of David; apostolic failures to Jesus after the multiplication of the loaves, or to St. Paul after his discourse at Athens, etc. It is by acquiring the habit of such a historical dialectic, in the manner of the Fathers of the Church, that young people will recognize today God's historical presence and transcendent support in their own lives.[27]

Finally, to call someone by name is to entrust a task to him, provide him with the occasion to realize his potentialities by action. To say "vocation" is to say "mission." This means that our catechesis must not only reach the intellect, but must lead to action and commitment in charity. It is not a question, here, of falling into a "neomoralism" of commitment, but rather of giving to all our teaching the dimension of Pentecost—that is, to reveal a God whose love desires to pour itself forth by associating our freedom with His infinite generosity.

It is no doubt absolutely necessary to propose to adolescents a wide range of activities; this is more particularly the role of education. It is the task of catechesis to unlock the knowledge of, and desire for, the true perspectives of a Christian vocation, which is always a personal mission in and for the Kingdom of God.

The threat of suffocation or anonymity and, on the other

[27] It should be noted that this method, which is so traditional in the Church, has been taken up on another level in Marxist teaching. Cf. Politzer, *Principes élémentaires de philosophie.*

hand, of worldly or Promethean intoxication, looms darkly over today's youth. Christmas, Easter and Pentecost must speak to them concretely of true life, of true mission. "If you but knew," Jesus told the Samaritan woman.

The Main Accents of Our Education

Chapter Eight

In the light of the broad outlines of our catechesis certain points of emphasis are called for in pedagogical practice today. Without claiming to say everything or to uncover the full extent of particular problems that arise in a given milieu, we shall try to focus on the essentials.

A Positive Education of Freedom

It is not enough to catechize. True freedom, that freedom which is communion with God for the sake of loving and creating, grows throughout the course of a long apprenticeship.

From what we have already said of the catechesis of freedom and vocation, the direction that a positive education of freedom will follow can readily be guessed. It must be pursued along two lines: we must teach true freedom both in the act of loving and in the act of creating. Discounting the follies of a crazy independence, we shall see to it that our whole educational system, the sanctions as well as regulations, foster in the best possible way the adolescents' generous and creative initiatives.

Is not the right method to suggest values, films, books, and encounters that will give the adolescent a desire for life? Over and above any method, however, we must know how to love with delicacy and humility, so that the other will feel comforted, inspired in his turn to love and respond. In short, it is a matter of knowing and calling each one by name, in order to entrust to him gradually that unique work by which he will become a better person and enrich the community. It matters little whether this work be painting, some apostolic activity, or supervising a sports team. To foster the uniqueness of another and discover that secret place where his freedom can become creation, gift and fullness is the greatest work that a teacher can accomplish.

Let us help young people to make an imprint on the things they touch, the house in which they live, the activities that are entrusted to them (the arrangement of a room, preparation of a feast, keeping the budget for a group, etc.).[1]

---

[1] Should we not, in this context, rethink our education to a proper use of money? Parents or teachers often discuss at meetings whether adolescents should be given pocket money, how much, etc. The young people usually think of this money as source of profit or of egoistic enjoyment.

This is a serious deviation, if we recall the importance of money in this world. But what are we doing to educate them to a sense of money which fosters spiritual growth and service of others? Do we educate them to see that, with their money, they can develop their human potential, keep house efficiently, serve the community? Such an education is one of the practical ways in which we can best help young people to make the transition from purely natural independence to positive freedom that creates values.

A certain group of boys from 15 to 18 who had organized with

Let us also teach them that true freedom is being open to others in the act of loving. Let us teach them to shape in a unique, personal way, in the Holy Spirit, their friendships and relations with others. Let us educate them to surmount egoistic jealousies and pleasures. In their reciprocal relationships they must come to know that true freedom of love which creates day by day, in God, the other's eternal vocation.

A young couple, recently married, stated emphatically: "You must tell young people that happiness and love are not something ready-made, something that you receive the way you receive a wedding present. It is something much finer that you make yourself, that you create together, day after day, in gropings, failures, and joys. We have understood that God has entrusted to us, has allowed us to construct, our happiness and our home. It is very important that they understand that God makes us the creators of our happiness."

In a world in the making there is no room for a Christian education that is closed, carefully shielded, or nurtured in a hothouse. If they would be faithful to their mission, educational institutions and youth groups must, from the first moments of adolescence, arouse and direct in joy and

---

their teacher a club was progressively led to invest the money they made in improving their club lounge, helping poor people, etc. The boys were happy with their new attitude toward money. Their freedom was now in the service of love and creativity.

Could we not suggest that the money they earn on certain jobs (waiting on tables, etc.) be spent for their education, helping a friend in need, etc.? This presupposes, of course, the presence of a true educator.

earnestness the need of young people to create and to love.[2] Will Catholic schools and youth movements become primarily bastions for defense, rather than the avant-garde of advance?[3]

Education of Awareness to the Other

The following incident illustrates the adolescents' drive toward the good:

"John, come here."

"Yes, Sir, what's the matter?"

"Would you like to earn some money?"

John comes running; then, after a moment: "How?"

Driven by his natural impulse John runs after the ideal image of himself with great rigor. He naïvely listens to the "gods of the blood" and has difficulty in focussing his attention on the God of Revelation, who speaks to him through the realism of facts. In our times when the concrete reality of persons and things is so important, it is particularly necessary to direct this spontaneous drive toward the good into a disinterested attentiveness to objective reality.

It is no easy task to help boys of 15 break through their egocentricity and overpowering sensations so that they can

[2] In this respect it should be considered quite normal in Catholic institutions that the adolescent from the age of 15 on contribute his creative share to the community, according to his vocation: student government, working on the school paper, captaining a sports team, charitable activities, etc.

[3] We must not oppose the two aspects. We should make it clear, however, that in our time, which extols freedom, we cannot educate young people without opening them to their mission—already at the age of 14/15—through humble, concrete tasks.

listen to and become aware of the other. But such an education has a twofold advantage: it is faithful to the purest
spirit of the Gospel and to the demands of the modern
world. We must pursue it with perseverance on all levels.
In our catechesis, in days of recollection, we must challenge
them to awareness of each other in their group life.

Since we shall have to re-establish the true scale of values,
we shall consider here the main accents of an education to
awareness in our schools and youth groups. Many of our
institutions bear witness to a set of values where obedience
to rules reigns supreme. The system of grades and punish-
ments essentially sanctions the technical breaking of the
law. As a result, it happens that groups of adolescents entrench themselves in a "Beat" egoism, in attitudes of jealousy and self-sufficiency, and remain quite undisturbed by
things that really matter. On the other hand, because they
know that the slightest breaking of silence is severely re-
primanded, they are careful not to trangress the law.

The monitor in charge of keeping order in the cafeteria
will see to it that the boys stay in line; but is he concerned
about their positive formation? Does he educate the adolescent in his relations with others and make him aware of
the demands of Christian courtesy at table: not to grab the
biggest piece of meat, passing the salt to his neighbor, etc.

There is the danger that gradually, without our being
aware of it, our insistence on a certain external order will
turn out good little smug, selfish conformist pagans. When
this is so the law, instead of leading to charity, will para-
doxically close the way to it.

All of our education must be for the sake of charity.

Thus, in the first place, it might be a good idea to ignore certain regulations which have become meaningless in the modern world and therefore appear to have no link with charity. Is it absolutely indispensable, for instance, to line up in silence before class? Is it necessary to insist on a uniform? Certain reforms are badly needed if we would make the law subservient to love, that is, to the students' spiritual development.[4]

Secondly, the true meaning of various rules or prohibitions should be explained regularly, and with reference to their end. Thus at home, instead of saying abruptly: "You must get up earlier. It's too late for breakfast now," let us explain firmly but with understanding: "Please try to be on time! Your mother can't cook just for you, she has work to do. Put yourself in her place!" We no longer have before us children, but adolescents who have the right to understand. They should gradually understand the law, not as arbitrary despotism but as fostering charity.

Finally, let us teach emphatically, at all times, the great unshakeable principles that are the foundation of moral conduct and collective discipline. Over and above his criticism of details, the adolescent needs to have explained to him these basic principles of life. They will be easy to understand, and he will not deny them in theory: the spirit of service, awareness of the other, friendship, the sense of God, respect for others, a concern for truth and justice, etc.

While we should certainly explain these foundations of

[4] We should a fortiori revise certain regulations, for instance, which seem to exist only to safeguard the school's prestige rather than foster the formation of the students.

Christian conduct in the classroom, we must above all make sure that our personal conduct, ways of reacting, punishing, of being joyful or sad, witness before young people to the primacy of these principles in our own lives. It should hurt us to see them kick a weak classmate, make fun of a poorly dressed boy, not listen to a question asked by another. Such attitudes should grieve us and be intolerable to us—far more than breaking the silence as they line up for class! And this should be apparent to those around us. Our faces easily express whatever we feel deeply, and the words we speak will now ring true.

One last factor: in this education to a Christian awareness of people and temporal realities the action of priests and religious must be complemented by that of lay people —here more than elsewhere.

By vocation, religious must maintain in their lives a certain detachment from earthly realities; this witness is, as we have seen, essential. The witness of lay people is no less so, if we want young people to learn the meaning of true Christian commitment. It is especially the laity's role to express the ways in which one's profession can be concretely viewed in the light of faith, how to act in the office, with one's neighbors at home, etc.[5]

[5] In religious institutions in particular, the presence of lay people, coming from outside, seems to us to be most necessary. If priests and religious have the full right to give the doctrinal and spiritual content of catechesis, they have less of a right, because of their vocation "outside the world," to show how Christianity pervades life in concrete earthly commitments. Who will show better than young lay people how one is to behave toward one's fellow workers? General principles are not enough. Lay people can show adolescents how to "touch" earthly realities.

In patiently educating the adolescent in small everyday details we shall prepare him for that awareness that will permit him to face in a Christian fashion the great realities of his profession and commitment to the world. Once purified from the subtle paganism of his instinctual drives, he will blossom forth in more conscious participation in God's infinite love for this time and world in which we live.

Education for the Christian Sense of the Event

"The event is the interior master," said Emmanuel Mounier.

We have shown how sensitive this technological generation is to facts, rather than to the pursuit of ideas and ideal perfection. We touch here a key point in the spiritual education of young people: we must teach them to recognize and welcome events as willed by God.

By "fact" or "event" we mean everything that is, everything that happens, e.g., an attack of appendicitis, failure in an exam, bad weather that upsets weekend plans, as much as the disturbing sensation of their instincts.

Today's generation is spontaneously sensitive to facts in their historical contingency, but is less ready to accept them as coming from God's hands or to perceive their supernatural significance. Far from it! The success so easily obtained through worldly means, the techniques of advertising, material comfort, etc., all these can harden man's heart in self-sufficiency, instead of opening him to a dialogue with God through daily events.

Through their power to dominate matter or the course

of events by ever greater scientific discoveries, men are in very real danger of considering persons and events only as "things" to be controlled, as realities whose secret one would learn in order to master them. What might have been a source of sanctity thus becomes a cause of failure.

A twofold emphasis is called for here. We must teach young people to accept the fact as providential, and we must help them to decipher its Christian significance.

Fatalism about exams, hidden disillusionment in the face of life—how many young people have lost the vitality of faith as they confront events! "What will be will be." No doubt life is hard for many, and they have not had that experience of love which gives joy of living. A sensitive formation is therefore called for.

This education requires, first, teachers who are close to the students, friendly and understanding. We are not going to explain to a boy who is ill that his sickness is a "gift from God." We can help him only if we first love him deeply. And if we do not have a personal knowledge of his suffering, we must help him carry his burden before we begin to speak.

Secondly, the Christian sense of the event requires a courageous catechesis on providence. Do we sufficiently proclaim Chapter 12 of St. Luke, on abandoning ourselves to the hands of the Father? One might doubt it. To boys worried about their future, to girls preoccupied with social success, we must proclaim the Kingdom and say: "Fear not!" Patiently, especially in moments of tension, at times of disillusionment or failure in school, we must be able to show them that God alone "makes a success" of man. The man who works courageously, according to God's will, is absolutely certain to succeed. To him who seeks first the Kingdom Jesus promised: "All these things shall be given you besides."

This decisive formula must be clearly understood by young people. On the one hand, we should show them that *to seek the Kingdom* is not necessarily to become a monk, but to work according to God's will. On the other hand, we must affirm that he who works thus is assured of success in life and in his relationships. We are not saying, of course, that God will grant man all his whims, nor that He will ratify all apparently legitimate temporal quests. We do insist, however, that the believer will be a success as son of God, an unprecedented supernatural success. We should reassure them, furthermore, that the Father's goodness will take care of them also in all that concerns the things of earth.

This is a difficult catechesis, but it is absolutely necessary if we would lead them beyond the spontaneity of small pagan commitments. In one form or another these evangelical precepts must resound again and again in their ears.

Finally, the Christian sense of the event demands that we accustom them to react to facts decisively. The new generation shuns romanticism. It tends to take life as it comes, without comment. Let us Christianize this trend of our times.

Let us teach them to put their vitality and sense of honor at the service of a humble realism, not of rebellion or deceit.

Today we experience the joy of a feast, the presence of a dear friend; tomorrow, hard work and perhaps failure. . . . Let them say Yes with all their soul, whether torn with pain or filled with wonder, for in both cases it is God who speaks.

Instead of insisting that they make resolutions which are too often idealistic or egocentric, let us awaken them to a humble fidelity toward daily reality. The climate of youth groups or educational institutions should foster this positive confrontation with life. Joy, a certain sportsmanship, an optimistic outlook, a bit of irony for romanticizing, the courageous acceptance of the 101 miseries of life: such attitudes will stimulate the Christian sense of life and of events.[6]

Let us not be too worried about their attachment to earthly mediations. If they practice generously the "asceticism of the event" God will bring about in His own good time the necessary detachment.

It is a difficult and delicate task to encourage adolescents today in the practice of mortifications exterior to their concrete situations, or urge them too strongly toward detachments which would encroach on God's own good time. They are naturally awkward and slow. If only they are faithful to events and to life, mortification and detachment will not be wanting. Is not this the message for our time of St. Thérèse of the Child Jesus?

Adolescents, as we have said, have the right to understand. This is a first point to keep in mind; but let us go further.

[6] This does not exclude, of course, understanding and kindness.

Today's young people learn, all through school, to understand the world of things in order to exploit and dominate it. The young carpenter knows the "language" of a piece of wood, its possibilities, and how to handle it in order to make a cabinet. The engineering student who presents his project to his professor knows the possibilities of matter and the secrets of its resistance.

It is more than ever necessary than we teach the value of history, the secrets of earthly effectiveness, the spiritual meaning of facts, the Christian sense of history, and the power of the Resurrection in the world, to these young people learning to know the weight of things. This is one of the points fraught with many consequences for their future as Christians. Unless we teach them the Christian meaning of history and events, an entire generation is likely to lose itself in doubt or in a vague natural religiosity.

From the very beginning Catholic Action has correctly understood this problem and has tried to meet it with an evangelical reflection about the concrete facts of existence. A similar effort must be made in catechesis. We should not necessarily follow the way of Catholic Action, which proceeds from below, i.e., from current facts and problems. However, even catechesis, which starts from above, must at all times throw light on daily life and conduct. The Revelation of the eternal ways of God, as "historicized" in time, must shed light on today's "small history."

Let us take some examples:

God invites Abraham to set out for the Promised Land. This means for the young person who hesitates to commit himself to his vocation that each time God calls He demands that we leave behind and set out; but God guarantees in return the Promised Land. . . .

Israel, a small people among the great nations of the earth, is comforted by the assurance of universal salvation. . . .

Jesus, during His public life, rejects quantity in favor of quality. . . .

Easter reveals the proclamation of mercy to all nations. . . . All these facts shed light on the contemporary scandal of the small number of men who form the visible part of the Church.

Not only catechesis, but also the spiritual talks customary in many Catholic schools or groups should attempt to throw light on daily events through the revelatory events of salvation history. Thus little by little the adolescent will be brought to recognize "his God," that God whose ways do not change from age to age, whose power never fails, once we have learned to recognize Him.

Let us stress three points in particular, three facts which young people see only with great difficulty through the eyes of faith:

They do not easily see in the light of faith their own drive to live. It is not enough to teach the adolescent to understand human or political events outside himself. We must also teach him, especially at the moment when his instincts threaten to sweep him along, to understand his own inner drives. We may even say that, for an adolescent, the great "fact of life" he must learn to understand is himself, all that he feels, thinks, suffers, and dreams.[7] This subjective fact of life can so easily remain pagan!

Our spiritual education should not only orient and regulates his drives, but, first and more basically, recognize their meaning and end. This is true of friendship, of the desire to succeed, to own a car, etc.[8] It is in this way that we shall prepare the young person to understand, tomorrow, that his love for his wife, his thirst to create, his relationships, are not purely carnal instincts, whims or chance, but are the holy irreplaceable will of the Lord.

Again, to accept, in faith, not only difficulties but limitation and failure is a great turning point in life. The adolescent prepares himself progressively for this by accepting failure in an exam, a disappointment in love, the impossibility of attaining ideal purity, etc.

The teacher must bring the light of Revelation to bear on all these small failures of daily life. But let him be careful! The catechesis of failure is a delicate matter, for it pre-

[7] It seems to us that this is one of the elements that distinguishes the approach of Catholic Action among adults and adolescents. The events of life are not the same. Among the latter they are primarily subjective, interior, often individual (e.g., boy-girl relationship), and require consequently an educational approach that is more delicate and discreet, less rational and more affective.

[8] In this sense the event is also, for adolescents, the mysterious awakening of biological forces that are strongly marked by the difference in sex. "To welcome God in the event" is to accept myself, in God, as man or woman. It is agreeing to this basic desire of God who calls me to realize myself, in Christ, through and in the conditioning which results from my sex. Nothing that makes a man of the adolescent boy, or a woman of the adolescent girl, is outside God's plan.

supposes not only a good verbal explanation, but above all the witness of an understanding presence. In times of failure man wants to able to believe in the love of another, more than he wants explanations.

Later, when he has personally experienced in his life the Passage of the Lord's goodness, he will be able to understand more easily the redemptive meaning of failure. He will need simply to refer to his own experience.[9] In addition to their objective meaning, the great deeds of God saving His people in history will have for him a subjective importance. In the meantime, however, he wants to be able to believe in someone.

Without belittling the value of necessary explanations, let us avoid the mistake of trying to solve everything, in the manner of Job's friends. Let us first of all be present. Let us listen and love. Evil is not a problem which one solves through knowledge. It is first of all a mystery on which light is shed through the acceptance of love.

It is true that any deep understanding of the meaning of failure requires a maturity which is beyond young people in general. Let us be patient, and let us for the time being educate them in concrete attitudes: docility, spiritual poverty, faith in our God's loving transcendence.

Thirdly, we should not be surprised that young people are slow in explicitly recognizing the Church. The event Christ-Church "is not revealed to you by flesh and blood,"

[9] We say, personal experience. It is obvious, of course, that the adolescent did not wait until he was 15 in order to experience God's goodness. Yet in childhood we cannot speak of a reflective subjective experience: God's kindness was taken for granted, in the framework of home and parents.

Jesus said to Peter, "but by My Father who is in heaven."

That Christ can be definitively united to this "humanity-Church" is absolutely unprecedented, supernatural. It is beyond man's reason and wisdom, even in the best adolescents! And yet, no true Christianity is possible without such a recognition in faith.

How can we help them come to this? First of all, let us use every opportunity in catechesis. Imitating the Fathers of the Church we should speak of the Institution-Church in personalist terms and analogies which will correspond to their subjective experience. We must help them enter into dialogue with the Person of Jesus, through His Body, the continuation of His risen Humanity. "This is He, that priest to whom you are going to confession. He makes the sign. He says to you: 'Your sins are forgiven. Go and sin no more.'" We should make frequent use of such a personal vocabulary, not only in our catechesis, but also in homilies and spiritual talks.

Secondly, we must not close our ears to a certain element of scandal. It is not by refusing to hear what everyone is saying about the Church that we shall answer the questions of young people. We must show them quite realistically that the Church, even though she is essentially holy and sanctified by the life of her Lord, still carries today a body of flesh weighed down by sin. Far from avoiding scandal, let us meet it head-on: we recognize Christ truly only on the day when we recognize Him wedded to, not a Church of angels, but a Church of sinners. On that day we recognize the Lord according to that which He is most profoundly: *mercy and salvation*.

We should not hide too much from young people the
shortcomings of priests and Christians in general. It is precisely here that, through grace, we must help them to see
Christ in His fullness, in His triumph, that is, in His mercy.
The Christ-Bridegroom did not wed a supraterrestrial
woman, but a woman of common lineage, the "girl of the
woods" of whom Ezechiel speaks. And men will say until
the end of time: "Behold, if he were God he would know
what sort of woman she is that touches him!" And again:
"How do you expect us to take this seriously? God, Yes;
but the priests, No!"

Now this is, precisely, the object of faith that we must
present to young people, not as the conclusion of a reasoning process, but as *mystery of love*. It is here, at this crucial
point, that we must make them aware of St. John's statement: "God so loved the world . . ."[10]

We insist on these points in order to forestall the temptation of giving young people an "angelic" picture of the
Church. It would be a mistake to protect them from her
human aspects. There are students who, momentarily dazzled by certain forms of liturgical life in a privileged community, leave the Church when they return to their parish
and find there no participation in the liturgy. Had these students really discovered the true face of the Bride of Christ,
when they refuse to recognize it beneath the rags of poverty
and mediocrity of her members? We know how essential

[10] This does not mean, of course, that we must sanction all sorts
of compromises. Cf. P. Babin, in *Actes du Congrès de l'enseignement Religieux* (Paris, 1960), "Catéchèse et insertion dans l'Eglise."

to their Christianity and to their sense of the Church are
genuine missionary and evangelical actions; but let us at the
same time show them the other side.

The spirituality of the event is the opposite of a spirituality of evasion. It demands so much lucidity and decision, so
much of the cross, so much exuberance also, that young
people cannot but go over to Him who has said: "I am the
Life."

Education to Universality

Giving young people a Christian sense of universality is
an important element of education today, because it takes
its human roots in current trends such as communication
with the entire world, possibilities of travel, international
relations, etc.

Such trends represent first of all a springboard for an
authentic missionary urge. Transcending the romantic fascination with faraway countries, young people who have been
educated in the charity of the Lord will be aware that the
Christian must be open to the entire world. Their natural
curiosity for other civilizations and foreign countries can become the object and concern of true charity, their desire for
contact with other peoples can become desire for a fraternal
gathering. Thus openness to the world is not only a natural
tendency. It is also Christian decision, under the impulse
of the Holy Spirit.

We can see in the taste for the universal a possibility for
a Christian way of life. By generously accepting openness of

spirit, by refusing the easy tranquillity of staying home, young people will counteract the limitations and imprisonment of purely earthly attractions. When two friends part in order to make contact with other cultures they break open the somewhat closed circle of their bonds of friendship. In this sense it is a good thing if young people, out of love for friendship and fullness of life, refuse to enclose themselves in a narrow point of view, in one jealous relationship, or in routine.

This breadth of spirit, this participation in the dimensions of the Spirit of God and willingness to be open to all of reality in the name of the Lord, will mortify attachments by putting them in their proper perspective.

Education for Communal and Social Life

Whereas the period of the Reformation gave the place of honor to values of individualism, today's world is becoming aware of its cohesion and unity, hence of social values. Scientific developments which reduce the distance between men and things simultaneously abolish the frontiers between men.

Adolescents, as we have seen, are not outside this trend of the times; they are becoming socialized. Deeply insecure, confused by revolution and the break with the past, by the gropings of their generation, they long for both the warmth of small communities human in size, and for collective responsibilities.

How can we help them find their place in this vast socialization of the world, and simultaneously assure the interiority of the human person, who is the unique subject of his acts and relationships? How can we answer, in a Christian perspective, their desire to be open to the world and at the same time their need for the small group? Let us suggest a few possibilities.

At this age, when the adolescent is in search of his personality, catechesis frequently used to present Christ to him as a model. It accented those aspects in Christ, however, which could help the adolescent in the affirmation of his personality, through a virtuous but individual way of life. It stressed much less those things which could help him develop as a "being-in-relation-to-others." Thus, the main accent was often on the ideal of the Person of Christ and on the harmony between his bodily and spiritual faculties. The adolescent then tried to reproduce in himself some traits of this model personality.

Should we not, rather, insist today on another aspect, namely, the wealth of Christ's personality in his relations with men? Should we not stress the harmonious interplay of His senses and spiritual powers which permitted Him to encounter and be open to other men, and which inspired His attitudes, words, and miracles? By becoming familiar with this face of Christ, adolescents will come to the unfolding of their personality in and through the human community. To become someone will be for them to exist through and for others, following Christ and in Christ.

Do we not also need to Christianize, in the formation of conscience, that whole naturalistic morality of popular magazines and books which extols formulae and techniques of success?[11]

Along the same lines, there is need for a Christian version of recent studies in social psychology. This would enable us to help each man find his place in the community true to his vocation, and to develop his own uniqueness within the whole, aware of his potentialities and limitations.[12]

Experiments along these lines made with boys of 15/16 were most encouraging. We noticed their great interest for everything that helps them find their place in the world of action and human relations. This is what we mean when we speak of educating them to their vocation in and for the Kingdom of God.

Youth groups or movements should try to establish true communities that are human in size. Not a conglomeration of individuals brought together by a rule and the necessities of life, but a gathering of persons in dialogue with each other, who, together, can accomplish a task in the service of others. These small communities must exist at all cost within those larger communities constituted by certain educational institutions, or structures such as the parish.

Here, the educator and youth leaders play a decisive role. A community is formed through a personal call, that is,

[11] *"How to Win Friends and Influence People*, etc. . . . . When shall we have books that teach us to put our human prestige, personal talents, temperament, desire to please, etc., at the service of the Lord?

[12] Cf. the works of Moreno. It is a good thing to help adolescents discover their talent for leadership, for binding a group together. Or, on the contrary, to make them aware of faults and weaknesses that stand in the way of their social—and Christian!—success.

around someone. It will endure to the extent to which this call arouses a free response, a forgetting of self in a task, a mission. The personal call of "someone," and the concrete mission or task which turns the group toward the outside and gives it its profound social meaning—these are the two elements that can form the basis of a youth group.

This "someone" around whom the group crystallizes may be a priest, a teacher, or, frequently, a young person of worth and prestige.[13] In the Christian context, this "animator" often plays a sort of prophetic role and mediates to the group not theories, but his own vision of reality, the radiation of his own life illuminated by the Holy Spirit.[14]

The common task which results from union among members of a group will safeguard the group's stability by eliminating internal criticisms and egoistic evasions. The task should be chosen, nevertheless, in the light of each one's capabilities and should be well suited to the dynamism of the "animator." In the light of faith, it should become a real Christian mission.

We should educate adolescents within the group in such a way that their friendships and preferences, their material choices, will never be the cause of quarrels or lack of balance. Nothing should divide the community (e.g., secrets between two people, egoistic isolation, cutting oneself off from others). The warmth of the bonds of friendship should

[13] We have seen clubs that were pagan to begin with grow in an explicitly Christian quality, thanks to one or two members who had the support of priests.

[14] Cf. A. Brien, "Les petites communautés, soutien de la foi," in Études (November, 1953).

always tend toward the goal, which is to raise the quality of the individual and to strengthen the community.

At its best the group life should find expression in prayer, the celebration of Penance,[15] and especially the Eucharist, which is the source and peak of all community life and of the apostolate.

Anyone who has experienced the intensity of prayer, charity, and apostolic dynamism of such communities knows that they are more necessary than ever for young people in this time of anonymity and solitude. Hence it is not surprising that other forms of education recede somewhat into the background and are replaced by a life lived in common and mutual support, by fraternal correction and the awareness of signs.[16]

---

[15] In certain countries today a more communal participation in the sacrament of Penance is being stressed. For instance: a group of young people, in preparation for the Mass of a great feast, or during Lent, come together to perform "an act of penance." The priest, at the beginning of the celebration, reads a passage from Scripture, as a call to repentance and conversion. This is followed by a time of silent reflection; then all recite the Confiteor. Next, all those who wish go to confession and receive the sacramental absolution. Even if not everyone goes to confession, the whole community is united at least in an interior spirit of conversion and, through the Confiteor, in the sacramental of Penance.

Such a celebration presupposes certain special physical conditions (e.g., a retreat, life in a Catholic school or parish group); but we can imagine its value for the group's Christian vitality, for mutual forgiveness and for unity in the Spirit of Jesus.

[16] A certain kind of spiritual direction seems on the wane today. We need spiritual direction, of course. We wish to point out, however, that when fraternal correction and true community once again recover the vitality they had in the first centuries of Christianity, the individual practice of spiritual direction becomes less urgent, precisely because the individual's needs are taken care of. This happens

Let us not be afraid that these small communities will express their life in too much "originality," deep joy, and genuine human warmth. This is not only a desperate need of our age but also a desire of God, who came to seal fraternal friendship with His presence. Let us not feel guilty when we see small groups taking shape. Let us, instead, see to it that these groups by their very nature become more and more open to apostolic concern in the service of mankind.

Experience has shown that young people who grow up in a dynamic and apostolic faith usually live in a community or small group. Even apart from youth, is this not an intrinsic demand of Christianity?

Education for a Personal Love of Jesus

Young people must learn to enter into a relationship with the "well-beloved Brother and Lord Jesus."[17] They should meet the Lord not only through His Mystical Body, as we often urge them today, but also through the unique reality of His Person. They must learn to speak to Him as one speaks to someone who is alive, with their whole being, with all their misery and needs.

We must take care here that collective education through

---

not so much in an individual relationship, as was the case among the Desert Fathers, but in the relationship with the living community. It will, by that very fact, lead to a deepening in the role which is properly the priest's in spiritual direction: in addition to administering the sacraments and to his pastoral duties in the community, the priest will have above all the doctrinal role of one who "animates" prophetically and teaches young people to discern the Spirit.

[17] This is one of the familiar phrases of Charles de Foucauld.

a liturgical life does not become anonymous regimentation. It should lead to the silence of adoration and personal encounter. This does not imply cutting oneself off from others. Modern men need to see that to pray is not making contact with God through a "direct line," but entering into dialogue with the living Word of the Lord. His Word establishes us necessarily in a relation with all our brothers, as well as with the heavenly Father in the Holy Spirit.

The Lord Jesus must not be an idea: this would be a terrible deformation. The man who says he loves his fiancée, but spends all his time at work without giving her times in which they are alone, is a liar. He does not love her.

We shall not elaborate further on this aspect. The means by which man can be introduced into a personal relationship with the Lord Jesus are being tried and studied constantly today. Nevertheless, we face in our education a certain danger of anonymity and depersonalization, even in our prayer.[18]

Education for Spiritual Poverty and Charity

Let us recall at the outset the great dangers which our education faces: the danger of self-sufficiency through imprisonment in pleasure, or through the intoxication of technological and earthly success; the danger of anxiety; the danger of egocentricity. A consideration of the last two is particularly important here.

[18] Young people today are still capable of an authentically contemplative prayer. Cf. Hans Urs von Balthasar, Prayer (New York: Sheed & Ward, 1962).

Today's adolescents, who seem to be so emancipated, are in fact curiously fearful and insecure. Among many there is a danger of obsession and introspection, of an exaggerated preoccupation with "getting themselves in hand." This can be explained only through fear of their weakness. Fear of doing something foolish creates an obsession and disarms them at the moment of struggle. The more a person lacks security and self-confidence, the more he runs the danger of obsession and egocentricity.

We should also take great care that mortification does not concentrate on an exaggerated preoccupation with self, but that it be open to others and lead to charity. Fasting, for example, is an excellent means for deadening one's vices. In insecure people, however, it can lead to obsession, to a dangerous preoccupation with certain vices. Consequently these vices become exaggerated and the exercise of charity is forgotten.

If we keep in mind these psychological and sociological factors it seems that education for asceticism should take place primarily on a threefold level: an asceticism that stresses charity; an asceticism that stresses poverty; an asceticism that is lived in community, in the Church.

Asceticism should be considered not as lessened vitality, but as fullness of life. In Christian terms this means, not interior brooding, but an intense practice of charity.

We shall make asceticism consist first of all in a direct education of charity toward the other. Asceticism should be centered on the other and lead to a forgetfulness of self. It should consist not so much in isolation or solitude, as in self-giving, delicacy in fraternal relationships, humble service, thoughtfulness, universal love, openness to others, etc.

Especially at certain times of the year (Lent, the great vigils), let us lead young people to a prayer which is very detached, deeply marked by authentic charity and devoid of self. We mean, not that pious muttering in which I speak to God of myself and think only about myself, but prayer that is profoundly God-centered and contemplative. Such prayer listens to God and gives itself to Him.

If self-sufficiency is the worst danger facing youth, as well as all of Christian life, our asceticism must lead to spiritual poverty, not to a purely human trust in ourselves.

We must make very clear to young people the profound meaning of this spiritual poverty. It is not a question of a sentimental choice or childish fear of life, but rather of recognizing themselves before God in an attitude of radical dependence, as creature, son or daughter, as sinner.

To achieve this, certain times of asceticism should in the first place be times of silence and listening to God, of abandonment into His hands, not times of action and creativity.

In this context we should mention the need for restoring Sunday as a time of gratitude, of listening to God, of mercy and offering.[19] Similarly, we should intensify our retreats and days of recollection, and encourage young people to make contact with the contemplative life as found in its fullness among monks. Their life appears as utter dependence on God, as though the "seventh day" had already begun once and for all.

---

[19] In addition to prayer we could also mention Lent and fasting, as acts through which one relearns dependence by acknowledging God as source of physical life. Cf. Régamey, *The Practice of Fasting.*

Disturbed by the pace of our world, yet excited and incapable of getting along wihout it, many young people desire more or less consciously a time in which they can be "made over" and blessed by the God of Life. And yet, restlessness is second nature to them. Asceticism, therefore, should help them be without a portable radio for a while, to go beyond their need for words and pictures—not in order to enter into a void from which man shrinks back in horror, but so as to become wholly attentive to God.

Finally, we should restore the original value to that basic asceticism of dependence on God that is the Christian meaning of the event.[20]

Given the growing dangers of obsession and egocentricity, it would be well to strengthen asceticism and prayer through the environment and support of the community, especially in relation to fasting and the practices of penance.

People who are insecure have a special need of collective exercises and resolutions. Let us remember that, traditionally, the goal of the monastery as community was to prepare men for a solitary Christian life. It is the community which little by little enables us to live in solitude.

Let us wisely direct adolescents. We may start them on the road of privations and secret penance only if they are capable of a life centered in God and not in themselves. Before learning individual practices of penance they should learn to live the Church's times of penance, according to their full meaning, from the Friday to the great fast days and Lent.

Furthermore, we should also consider each one's temper-

[20] See above, pp. 232 ff.

ament. To teach adolescents to recognize their weak spots, their individual temperament, is to teach them to accept who they are before God, as grace of God.

Those who are high strung, for instance, are made for a balance of tension and drive, not for immobility and rest. For them, the dangers and limitations of earthly mediations will find rest above all in the Passion of Jesus, in a great childhood of heart, and in boundless trust. Unemotional temperaments, on the other hand, can afford to impose on themselves a greater rigor in observing laws, etc.

These are delicate problems. Only obedience and humble reference to the community will save us from illusions which often conceal a subtle pride.

Conclusion

Throughout these pedagogical and pastoral considerations we have tried to throw light on the main lines of a Christian education to human and temporal values.

In theory we have made a distinction between catechesis and education; but the reader will have noticed that, in practice, these two realities are inseparable, especially in the case of young people whose affective life is so strong.

Over and above the studies, orientations, and means indicated, each teacher will perhaps have felt the magnitude and difficulty of the task. To Christianize human and earthly values is not an easy undertaking. The spirituality of "Paschal joy" is at the heart of the cross and death. Should we not prepare young people to suffer greatly, so that they may become fully human? We must teach them to die, that is, to give without counting the cost, for the sake of all their potentialities.

Instead of driving them to amusement and a dissipation of energy, let us launch them on the great adventure of life that is communion with the Risen Lord.

In the "silent revolution" which today's youth is effecting, can the voice of the Church, Mother and source of true Life, fail to speak?